SAM ADEYEMI

ISBN Paperback: 978-1-943485-06-2
ISBN Ebook: 978-1-943485-05-5

All scripture quotations, unless otherwise indicated, are taken from the New King James Version.

Scripture quotations marked (AMP) are taken from the Amplified Bible.

The Parable Of Dollars: *Proven Strategies for Your Financial Success*

First Published 2001

Printed in the United States of America

CONTENTS

ACKNOWLEDGMENTS

I wish to acknowledge the inputs of all the exceptional people who have contributed to the publishing of all the editions of this book. This includes all the staff at Pneuma Publishing Company and Daystar Christian Centre, who have not only helped in publishing the title, but have also helped to test the principles.

I appreciate also our hardworking staff at Success Power and the talented people at GodKulture.

I can always count on my family's support for my endless flow of projects. My sincere gratitude to my sweetheart, Adenike, and to our lovely children: Sophie, David and Adora. I appreciate their love, patience and brilliant ideas always.

INTRODUCTION

The Parable of Talents is one of the most prominent parables of Christ. The word "talent" connotes an inherent gift or ability. My assumption for a long time was that the parable was a teaching on the stewardship of our God-given gifts and abilities. However, it later dawned on me that the talent also refers to a currency used in the days of Christ just as the dollar is an international currency in our days. This was the meaning Christ employed in the parable. While the parable is about our stewardship of the resources God has given us, it is based on financial management principles. How could we understand the parable if we don't understand the financial principles? The parable is replete with powerful principles for financial success.

I have written this book with a burden in my heart. Israel's deliverance from slavery in Egypt was not complete without economic freedom. Your deliverance from the kingdom of darkness is also not complete without economic freedom. My intention as I write this book is that on one hand it would be a reminder of the things you may have learned on finances from the Bible and, on the other hand, it would ignite a spark in you that will motivate you to take practical steps towards proactive wealth creation.

In these pages, I go a little beyond conventional teachings on giving to dwell more on how to cultivate wealth-building habits like saving, investing and becoming an entrepreneur. I conclude it all with some powerful principles on building wealth supernaturally through addiction to the Kingdom of God.

This book is destined to raise financial giants. This is the third revision and the eight printing. God has used it to birth outstanding testimonies already. Yours will be next. When you follow the principles presented in it, you will cross over to the other side of lack. You will be the bank owner, the landlord, the business owner, and the real estate mogul. I pray that it will be for you a first step on the ladder of wealth; and if you are already on the ladder, that it will result in your movement to a higher level. I wait to share in your wonderful testimony of change!

CHAPTER
1
THE PARABLE OF DOLLARS

The parable that is the subject of our discussion is often referred to as 'The Parable of Talents.' For the purpose of this book, I will refer to it as 'The Parable of Dollars,' as it will be easier for you to relate to the dollar as an international currency.

"For the kingdom of heaven is like a man traveling to a far country, who called his own servants, and delivered his goods to them."[1]

First of all, I want you to note the fact that this parable is about money. For a long time after I became a born again Christian, all the sermons I heard preached on this parable were about serving God with our gifts and talents. But in studying the passage, I discovered that the word "talent" was simply the currency at the time Jesus used this parable. Although we could learn other things from this parable, I see it as a treasure house of powerful financial principles. It is a whole package on financial success. As you read, I know you are about to step into a new level in your finances.

Jesus said; "For the kingdom of heaven is like a man traveling to a far country, who called his own servants, and delivered his goods to them."[2] He was trying to show us how the kingdom of heaven operates. The goods were not the goods of the servants but that of the master.

The starting point of financial breakthrough is for you to realize that you are God's steward. The money you have is not yours. It is something committed to your trust by the actual owner. It is a breakthrough when you understand that there is nothing you have that you have not received from God. You must handle your finances as God's steward. Always keep in mind that you own nothing really. You have simply been put in charge of things. When you are conscious of your stewardship, you will always consult the real owner, God, before making decisions on your finances. You will always be accountable to Him.

Many of us run our finances without involving God the way we ought to. Yet He is the one who best understands the principles of financial success. He said, "I am the Lord that teaches you to profit and leads you in the way that you should go."[3] The Psalmist said; "The Lord is my Shepherd, I shall not want."[4] One of the areas the Lord wants to transform in your life is your finance. If you follow God's leading, you won't lack.

God is the owner of your life. If He withdraws His breath from you now, you would not have anything left. You may say, "I'm the owner of my life and I can do anything I like with it." But saying that still does not make it true. It is not yours. Someone gave it to you. There is nothing you have that you have not received. So, in reality, it is not your life. You need to ask the giver of your life what to do with it.

When you say, "my time," remember that it is not yours. It is His. That is why David said; "My times are in your hands."[5] Moses had to ask God to "teach us how to number our days so that we may apply our hearts to wisdom." [6] You are only a steward of what God has given you. Have that attitude with respect to your finances.

USE WHAT YOU HAVE

God somehow gets across the initial funds that each person needs to start with financially. The master in this parable gave something to each of his servants illustrating how God gives to everyone something they can start with.

"And to one he gave five talents, to another two, and to another one; to each according to his own ability; and immediately he went on a journey."

Your physical strength, for instance, is a resource you can start with. Other examples of the resources God gives are your mental abilities, gifts, ideas, relationships and even the income you are getting today no matter how small. When you understand this, you will not feel as if you do not have something to start with. Do not look too far for what God will use to give you a financial breakthrough. It is already around you.

Ask God to help you recognize it. Everyone has talents. But notice that the master gave everyone according to his own ability. What kind of ability is referred to here? It is the ability to manage finances well. The Lord weighs your capacity. He will not give you money that will kill you. He will give you only what you can handle.

Remember Jesus said, "No man pours new wine into old wineskins." [7] If you pour new wine into an old wineskin, the old wineskin will be destroyed, wasting the wine. Since God does not waste His resources, He has got to look at what you have the capacity to handle per time. The more you increase in your ability to manage funds very well, the more the Lord will increase the flow of funds in your direction.

MULTIPLY YOUR MONEY

"Then he who had received the five talents went and traded with them and made another five talents." [8]

I want to emphasize that you develop the ability to multiply money. With most people, when money gets into their hands, it reduces in quantity. But with some others, it multiplies when it reaches their hands. Financial success and wealth is not all about spending money; it is about making it.

Unfortunately, what most of us know about finances was picked up while we were growing up. We were not taught how to make money in school. Most of our money habits were picked up from home. We learned how to spend money not how to make it. You must develop the ability to make money. The man with the five talents traded with what he was given.

We could be so materialistic that we use material things to define success: the size of one's car, the size of one's house, electronic gadgets and so on. The accumulation of material things is what some consider as wealth. But that is not all there is to wealth. Material wealth is one of the expressions of wealth, and we need to know how to create it. You have to start by being able to make money like the servant with the five talents.

Take note of the word "trade." What does it mean to trade? Trading is simply offering something at a price that will earn you a profit. So, the question here is; 'what are you selling?' What do you have to offer? There must be a product or a service that you are offering from which you hope to get some returns.

Paying tithes, praying, waiting and expecting that somebody will suddenly knock on your door with money in his hands are not enough. God certainly blesses people this way but this is the exception rather than the norm, though those are the kinds of testimonies some prefer. Here is a scenario you probably dream about: You are about to enter your car when a fellow runs up to you and asks: "Are you Mr. James?" You say: "Yes." And the person says: "Praise the Lord; you are the one I saw in my dream. An angel of the Lord appeared to me, showed me your picture and said I should give you this check for $100, 000."

When you hear a testimony like this you say: "That is God!" Yes, He does that sometimes. However, generally, you get money in exchange for meeting people's needs through products and services.

"And likewise he who had received two gained two more also. But he who had received one went and dug in the ground and hid his Lord's money." [9]

If you are in your 20s or 30s and you do not want to be broke at the age of 60, do something now. It is almost too late to start when you turn fifty or sixty. Your money habits today determine your financial future. Many who are wealthy today started working at it at an early age. Some saved up during their college years in order to own real estate and now they are reaping good money. Some bought shares in companies and now they own stocks and get good dividends. And some established small businesses.

Financial success is progressive. Until you can manage the hundreds you have, you are not prepared to handle the thousands and then the millions. Until you pass the test at one level, God will not allow you to advance to the next level. He says: "You have been faithful over a few things, I will make you ruler over many things." [10]

God predicts what you will do with the millions by what you do with the hundreds. He knows it and He sees you. If you are squandering the seemingly small amounts now, He knows you will squander the millions. If you are not paying tithes on $2,800, He knows you will not pay your tithe on $2.8 million. If you are generous with a little, you will be generous with much.

Now let us consider the servant who received one talent. He said: "Lord I knew you to be a hard man reaping where you haven't sown and gathering where you have not scattered seed." [11] What was the man's excuse for not multiplying money? He believed that his master was a hard man who loved to reap where he did not sow and who loved to gather where he did not scatter. This explains the problem with a lot of poor people. They are very angry with the rich. You need to realize that the people who make the most money in any business are not the people who work the hardest physically.

Here is an illustration. If you have one million shares in Exxon Mobil and a dividend of $1 per share is declared, your dividend is $1m. You get $1m for owning shares though you do not work for Mobil. You just own the shares. Someone else works as an office assistant at Exxon Mobil and gets paid $1,000 monthly.

This person would have made just $12,000 in a year. So who gets more money? The man who does not work with Mobil, but owns Mobil shares earns more. The man that is not working at Exxon Mobil is getting more money than the one who is working.

This is what the servant observed about his master. He noticed that the man was busy collecting money from places where he was not working. His summary was that he was a hard man. He was not a hard man at all. Rather, he was sensible. He was a man with financial intelligence who knew how to make other people work for him.

The servant also said; "And I was afraid, and went and hid your talent in the ground. Look, there you have what is yours."[12] The servant was overcome by fear! In the book, The Instant Millionaire by Mark Fisher,[13] the story is told of a young man who went to a millionaire and asked to be taught the secrets of success. The millionaire replied, "Okay, but before I share the secrets with you, you have to write a check of $25,000 to me that would be cashable in 30 days." The young man screamed: "Where do you expect me to get that?" His monthly paycheck at that time was just $1,000. "You just sign the check and give it to me," replied the old man. The older man was trying to teach the young man an important lesson. Your financial breakthrough begins when you box yourself in and give yourself no option but to produce a specific amount of money. All your faculties will be activated. Every time you avoid challenges, you avoid your breakthrough.

The lazy servant said he was afraid: afraid to take a plunge. Just like some are afraid to leave their meager paychecks in pursuit of a business they are not sure of. Insecurity, inferiority complex and a victim mentality are things that keep a lot of people from taking the steps that will give them the breakthrough they desire.

"But his lord answered and said to him, You wicked and lazy servant, you knew that I reap where I have not sown, and gather where I have not scattered seed…"[14]

My conclusion from this is that there are people in the church who refuse to multiply money because they are not willing to stretch themselves. They say things like: "I am okay. I am not covetous. I just need enough to be comfortable. I am okay the way I am." Jesus said that those who refuse to multiply money are wicked and lazy. Why would Jesus say that? It is because they are living a twisted and selfish life.

This is my suggestion: If you are not going to make a lot of money for your own sake, please make it for the sake of many that are suffering and souls that need to be saved. Once you get to the level where you are satisfied and don't need the rest of your money, just bring it to church. The church will make good use of it.

I am always disturbed when I hear adverts on the radio, or see them on television and billboards all over the country, advertising liquor and cigarettes. I tell myself that since the gospel of Jesus is the solution that everybody needs, then I should be as bold as those selling liquor and cigarettes. If their "gospel" comes up every thirty minutes, the gospel of Christ should come up every thirty seconds. People need Jesus not liquor or cigarettes.

INVEST YOUR MONEY IN THE BANK

"So you ought to have deposited my money with the bankers, and at my coming I would have received back my own with interest."[15]

The master of the servants said putting money in the bank was the minimum investment the servant could have done. I am not talking about the savings account. The interest you earn on a savings account is not multiplication. It is a reduction of your money. By the time you factor in inflation at the end of one year and add the interest on it, you will realize that the rate of inflation is higher than the interest your money has earned; hence you would have lost money in real terms.

I am definitely not talking about savings. I am talking about negotiating with your banker and putting some money in a fixed deposit account. God will definitely channel money in your direction once you decide to follow His principles.

Money will always flow away from those who don't know how to treat it well to those who do. Let me put it another way; it is poor people that make rich people rich. Money flows from tenants to landlords, from commuters to transportation companies and from those who buy to those who sell. Though done indirectly, it is the tenant that pays the tuition of the landlord's children. Whenever tuition increases in school, the landlord also increases the rent. From today, you won't be on the losing end. You will be on the prospering side.

You will find out that financially, people can be grouped into two camps: The buyers and the sellers. Make sure that what you are selling is more than what you are buying. That is how you grow wealthy. If you are buying more than you are selling, you will be a debtor. If you are consuming more than you are producing, you cannot build wealth. Make sure you have something other people need to buy. Make sure what they are buying from you is more than what you are buying from others.

"For to everyone who has, more will be given, and he will have abundance, but from him who does not have, even what he has will be taken away."[16]

He "who has" means "he who multiplies his money." Jesus was talking about the person who had five and multiplied it to ten, or the one who had two and multiplied it to four. "He who has not" is the person who refuses to multiply money. I am challenging you to classify yourself. Choose which group you belong to. Notice what he said about those who multiply money; they will have abundance. That is the picture I have about you. I see you moving into abundance. I see God stepping into your financial affairs.

"And cast the unprofitable servant into the outer darkness. There will be weeping and gnashing of teeth."[17]

Let me say this: Pain is inevitable. In this life, you will experience pain. There are two types: The pain of discipline and the pain of regret. If you pay now, you will play later, but if you play now, you will pay later. It is better to experience the pain of discipline now. What is the pain I am talking about? It is the pain of being productive. It is the pain of trading when or where it is not convenient. Just make sure you are making some profit.

It may be tough but do not quit. I am describing the pain of going to school to study and staying there till you see it through. It is the pains of not spending all the money you have now, refusing to satisfy all your cravings.

However, it is better to experience that pain now than to experience the pain of regret later. Jesus said that in the outer darkness, what you get is weeping and gnashing of teeth. That will not be your situation. Take note of the following steps and study them. Read through each item and then decide what you are going to do.

$$\boxed{\text{ACTION PLAN}}$$

USING WHAT YOU HAVE

Some call it talent, some call it ability, still, some call it an inborn trait, but whatever it is, you can use it to your advantage.

The starting point for financial breakthrough is for you to realize that you are only God's steward. The money you have is really not yours but something committed to your trust by the real owner.

It is a breakthrough when you understand that there is nothing you have that you have not received. You must handle your finances as God's steward. It is not yours; you are simply put in charge of it. When you are conscious of your stewardship, you will always consult the real owner, God, before making decisions on your finances. You will always be accountable to Him.

1. What is your area of strength/talent?

....

2. How do you know that it is your strength?

....

....

....

3. Is it working for you?

....

4. What do people say makes you stand out?

....

5. What are you doing now? And what would you rather be doing if money was not an issue and you are assured of success?

....

....

....

....

6. Write out clearly and concisely all the information in steps 1-5 above

....

....

....

....

7. What is your conclusion?

....

....

8. Which of these - education, money, relationship, skill, assets and so on, do you have that can be of help?

....

....

....

MONEY MATTERS

1. If you received a financial miracle, how would you handle it? (Write about six things)

....

....

....

....

....

....

2. Narrow your answers above down to two and give reasons.

....

....

3. What investment opportunities are open to you?

....

....

4. How would you like to take advantage of them?

....

....

Well, financial progress does not happen by chance or by wishing. You should understand that just wishing your finances were better will not get you anywhere. Remember the popular adage: "If wishes were horses, beggars will ride."

You must commit yourself to a definite plan of action. Let us go on.

1. What product or service are you offering presently?

....

....

2. What is your current income monthly or annually?

....

3. How much do you have in savings?

....

4. How much do you have in investment accounts?

....

5. Which do you prefer: To work for money or that money works for you?

....

6. Are you from a rich, lower or middle-income background?

....

7. If you were asked to get $1 million within the next month, how would you feel and how would you get it?

....

....

Money flows away from those who do not know how to treat it well to those who know how to treat it well. Make up your mind to change your attitude towards money so it can flow towards you.

CHAPTER
2
WEALTH MENTALITY

The major difference between the poor and the rich is in who they are, not just what they do or have. Lots of people assume that when they do what rich people do and acquire what rich people have, they would be rich. However, people who have tried that have discovered that it is a wrong assumption.

The major difference between the rich and the poor is in who they are. It is internal. It is not just about doing or having; it is about being. Material things cannot change who you are; they only give expressions to who you are. The beginning of wealth is in the heart.

"For as he thinks in his heart, so is he."[1]

Solomon, the biblical king who was reputed to have been the wealthiest person in the Old Testament, said also;
"As in water, face reflects face, so a man's heart reveals the man."[2]

When you look into water, you see your face. The water can only show you what you have presented to it. Likewise, what is in your heart is what you will give expression to. You will never get a better situation on your outside than you have on your inside. The quality of your life will not appreciate beyond the quality of your heart.

The first law of success is: "First within, then without."

Jesus expressed the same principle as Solomon this way:
"The good man from his inner good treasure flings forth good things, and the evil man out of his inner evil storehouse flings forth evil things."[3]

Prosperity and poverty are flung out of the heart the same way. So, you have to be deliberate about watching the state of your heart.

"Keep your heart with all diligence, because out of it spring the issues of life."[4]

Many people believe that the kind of hard work that would bring wealth is physical labor. But this is not entirely true. The statement above shows us where the work is: in the heart. Change the state of your heart. Re-program your mind! That is where the real hard work is, for creating wealth.

Jesus said no man puts new wine into old wine bottles. Heaven has something new to pour into your life. Please note that it is not your prayer that will make God decide to pour those things into your life. He decided that those things are yours even before you were born. It is changing your capacity to receive that will allow Him to pour those things into your life.

"And no one puts new wine into old wineskins; or else the new wine will burst the wine-skins and be spilled, and the wineskins will be ruined."[5]

You became qualified to possess them when you gave your life to Christ; but they cannot be released beyond your capacity to receive.

So, until your financial capacity increases, God will not increase the flow of supplies in your direction. He has new things to pour in, but He is expecting some change in your vessel, that is, your heart.

There is a story of a young man who went fishing. Whenever he caught a fish, he would measure the fish with a stick. If the fish happened to be shorter than the stick or was same length, he would drop the fish into his bucket. However, if the fish was longer than the stick, he threw the fish back into the river. When his friend asked him why, he explained that the stick was the measurement of his frying pan at home. Hence, any fish longer than the stick could not fit into his frying pan and was considered a waste!

UNTIL YOUR FINANCIAL CAPACITY INCREASES, GOD WILL NOT INCREASE THE FLOW OF SUPPLIES IN YOUR DIRECTION.

This is an example of how the human mind operates. Whenever anything comes that one's mind does not have the capacity to contain, it repels the idea. Jesus does not waste His resources. Heaven will not pour new wine into old wine skins. Doing so will imply a waste of both the skin and the wine.

Likewise, new levels of blessing poured into unready vessels could become a curse rather than the intended blessing. Instead of blessing your life, it will end up putting you under pressure and stress. Therefore, the core of the message is that the container must change so that new wine can be poured into it.

Until we change, nothing changes. Everything begins from the heart. The journey from rags to riches, from grass to grace, from poverty to prosperity is an internal trip.

According to James Allen; "You cannot travel within and standstill without."

UNTIL WE CHANGE, NOTHING CHANGES. EVERYTHING BEGINS FROM THE HEART.

You do not have any business trying to change situations and circumstances. That is God's business. Your business is to change your attitude and thinking pattern, to ensure that you are traveling and gaining speed on the inside. Once you move inside, your outside is compelled to move.

What do you do to change the state of your heart? Change your thinking. The average person experiences frustration because he wants to change what he does not have the power to change. You can change your complexion but it does not change your race. Also, stop trying to change other people. Things will not necessarily change for you if others change. We try to change situations and circumstances, yet it is easier to change ourselves than to change other people. Meanwhile, the responsibility God has given us is to change ourselves.

When you alter your attitude towards other people, they will alter their attitudes towards you. When you alter your attitude towards circumstances, circumstances will begin to respond to your advantage. That is why it is said that your attitude determines your altitude. A major difference between the rich and the poor is in the way they think. They think differently. So the question is: "How do you think?"

"And do not be conformed to this world but be transformed by the renewing of your mind."[6]

In your finances, you will literally experience transformation if you renew your mind and change your thinking. The scripture above is divided into two parts. The first part: "Do not be conformed" infers that you should challenge conventional thinking. When you realize that most people are poor, it is good for you to make up your mind that you won't think the way they think. If you want to be rich, you must stand out in your thought process. You cannot think the way the majority thinks because their thinking is not getting them anywhere. Do not do things because that is the way most people do it.

MAXIMS OF CONVENTIONAL THINKERS

A Nigerian proverb says: "Let us do it the way it has always been done, so that it can be the way it has always been." The question is: "How has it been?" If they have been doing it the way it has always been done and there is still so much poverty around, then this proverb does not apply to you.

You should note that only few people could mentor you financially. There aren't so many rich people around. Therefore, you need to challenge conventional thinking and break free from those maxims and sayings because they have the ability to program your mind negatively.

Just decide that you are not going to travel the same road with everybody else. Stand out.

I have discovered that even when you do not know what the Bible says about a situation, if you decide not to travel in the direction the majority is headed, you are likely to be right. So challenge conventional thinking. When people say: "Do not bite more than you can chew," decide to bite more than you can chew knowing that God will help you chew it.

Lots of people are just managing to go on with little or no accomplishments because of the fear of taking risks.

THE AVERAGE PERSON EXPERIENCES FRUSTRATION BECAUSE HE WANTS TO CHANGE WHAT HE DOES NOT HAVE THE POWER TO CHANGE.

They are afraid to aim for big things. Bite more than you can chew. If all you are attempting to do is all that you can accomplish by yourself, then you do not need God.

When you are told; "If you try it, you will face the music." I advise that you try it and face the music. Eventually you will conduct the choir! Everybody says, "Take care." For once, refuse to take care. Take a chance! If you take care all your life, you may never accomplish anything big.

Dare to do something. Get on with a project such that right in the middle of it, you will have to cry out to God to help you. That is when God comes in. Jump on the water like Peter did, and if you sink, God will hold you.

...FACE THE MUSIC, EVENTUALLY, YOU WILL CONDUCT THE CHOIR!

Some say: "A bird in hand is worth two in the bush." That could be true sometimes, but it could also be poverty thinking. Why should you settle for one bird, when there are thousands of birds flying around in the bush? You do not fish in the stream behind your house when you want to catch a whale. You go where the whales are! Think the way rich people think, so that you can do the things they do. They take big risks.

The devil has so much influenced the thinking of the church that he has even used the scriptures to program us for poverty. For a long time, the church believed that the poorer you were, the holier you were. We believed poverty was synonymous with piety. Nothing could be further from the truth. It was so bad that people started misquoting scriptures from the pulpit.

Some have claimed that the Bible says, "Money is the root of all evil," when the Bible actually says: "The love of money is the root of all evil."[7] It is your relationship with money that is the problem. Money is neither good nor bad. It is neutral. It takes after the character of its owner.

PULLING DOWN THE STRONGHOLDS

"For though we walk in the flesh, we do not war according to the flesh. For the weapons of our warfare are not carnal but mighty in God for pulling down strongholds. Casting down arguments and every high thing that exalts itself against the knowledge of God, bringing every thought into captivity to the obedience of Christ."[8]

What are strongholds? A stronghold is a military term that refers to a wall built to prevent the enemy from coming in. You do not just push a stronghold with your finger and tip it over. In modern times, hand grenades and missiles are used to pull down strongholds. That is how challenging it is to change your thinking.

The average person is in love with his own opinion. We all romance our convictions. It was not easy for me to breakthrough from the mentality of pastoring a small church to the mentality of pastoring a large church.

If you stay around rich people, it is certain that they will change your thinking pattern. They will stretch your mind. That is what usually scares people from rich men. When I seek advice from my mentors, the things they tell me to do are usually completely different from what I think I need to do to succeed.

If you are still struggling with financial independence, many of the things you know about money may be assumptions and assumptions are the lowest level of knowledge. I thought I knew what it would take to build a large church, but my mentor told me to stop struggling to bring big names to our church to attract a large crowd. I was shocked. I had always thought that when a pastor invites powerful guest speakers, he pulls a large crowd that eventually becomes his church members.

However, my mentor helped me understand that no church can outgrow its pastor. Thus, every church must grow from the heart of the pastor. He advised me to strive to be the person people would want to listen to. That was sound advice, but a total departure from what I had in mind. There was a time I thought my financial prosperity was tied to going to preach abroad and earning a lot of foreign exchange, but my mentor said, "Stay on your job; prosperity is not from abroad, but from above." Of course, I did not want to do that but I had to.

I admit that it is not easy to change one's thinking pattern. It is hard work. If you are part of a community or nation that has a strong belief in the power of witchcraft, the most critical witches and wizards you need to fight are the thoughts inside you and not in any coven. Having understood the impact of the power of thoughts on destiny, I have come to the conclusion that if the witch inside you (your thinking) cannot kill you, the one in the coven cannot kill you either. Of course witches do exist, but if you are born-again and Spirit-filled, a witch is no challenge to you.

The witch is only as powerful as you make her to be. If you are a believer, the devil is a non-entity relative to you. You know that if you kill all the devils in the world and you do not change your thinking, you still will not move an inch forward. So use the Word of God to change your thinking.

The barriers and limitations you are trying to break are inside you. The Bible is the book of opportunities. It sees opportunities where people see problems, speaks life when others speak death, sees miracles where others see obstacles, and sees abundance where others see scarcity. You can never be poor if you:

* Line up your thinking with the Bible.
* Read the books rich people write.
* Associate with rich people.
* Are careful about those who advise you.

When you act based on assumptions instead of knowledge you miss the connecting point with your breakthrough. It happened that a Syrian army general, Naaman, went to seek Elisha to heal his leprosy.[9] Elisha asked his servant to go and tell Naaman to wash in River Jordan. Naaman became angry. He had assumed that Elisha would perform a spectacular miracle. He said that he expected the prophet to come out, call on God and wave his hand over the leprosy. That was his problem; his thinking was faulty. If he knew how to cure leprosy this much, why did he come all the way from his country?

The level of thinking that brought us to where we are cannot carry us beyond where we are. We need to change the way we think to move us higher than our current level. Napoleon Hill titled his book: "Think and Grow Rich," not "work and grow rich," or "struggle and grow rich." Dr. David Oyedepo, my mentor, says: "If you don't think, you will stink."

Poor people think it takes money to make money. Rich people think otherwise. They know it takes ideas. Poor people work for money; rich people make their money work for them. Make a commitment to change your thinking - to pay the price no matter the cost.

POOR PEOPLE WORK FOR MONEY; RICH PEOPLE MAKE THEIR MONEY WORK FOR THEM.

Dr. Mike Murdock recommended that if you are serious about your finances, the number of books you have about finances must be equal to your age. Hence, if you are forty years old, you should have forty books on finances.

Most poor believers believe that prayer and fasting would bring breakthroughs. Prayer and fasting could bring the power of God. However, if your thinking does not change, your financial prosperity will only continue to accumulate in the spirit realm and would not be able to manifest physically until you change.

It is not sufficient for you to give tithes and offerings to make progress financially. There has been a little bit more increase in revelation. Pay your tithes, give your offerings, and then, think straight. Think plenty and think abundance. You do not recognize money with your physical eyes but with your mind, so get financial intelligence.

Think about this: imagine someone who needs to keep an appointment and has to take a bus but ends up arriving late for the appointment because there were few buses and lots of people waiting to board before him. He could react to this by saying, "I do not even know what's happening in this city, it's so difficult to get a bus. Life is just too hard in this city." Yet another person comes and sees the crowd with no bus in sight and immediately his mind recognizes that there is an opportunity to make money by going into the transport business. He decides to seize this opportunity by buying a bus. He concludes: "I will solve the problem of transportation in this city and make money from the fares people will pay."

The difference between these two people is their thinking. One sees a problem while the other sees an opportunity. Receive the grace to recognize opportunities in Jesus name. Make a commitment to change your thinking. Prepare yourself as a new wineskin ready to receive the new wine.

GET HUNGRY

"No one, having drunk old wine, immediately desires new; for he says, 'the old is better.'" [10]

God always wants to do something new in our lives but the average person is satisfied too soon. Don't say the old days were better, because there is a new level. Success is not a destination, it is a journey and you are not yet there. It is too early to arrive now; too soon to be living in your last house, driving your last car or being on your last job. God wants to pour something in; but He wants to know your capacity to receive before He pours it. He cannot pour it, until you change and increase in capacity.

SUCCESS IS NOT A DESTINATION, IT IS A JOURNEY.

We used to think God did not have enough, but now we know that He has abundance of new wine. But the condition is that we must have the capacity to receive it. The principle is this: The state of your heart determines your state on the earth. The difference between the poor and the rich is not in what they do or what they have but in the quality of their hearts.

CONTROL YOUR EMOTIONS

Gain control over your emotions. They affect the state of your finances because they affect your thinking and who you are. I know that in the church today, we would rather have someone lay hands on us for our situations to change, but how many people have changed without discipline?

It disturbs me because I know that the best way to enjoy the miracles of God is to consistently build your life on the principles of God. This guarantees consistent results. I am sure you know that planting seeds and having a good harvest is a principle, but praying that God should give you a harvest without planting seeds is leaving your life to chance.

Your success will be more predictable when you sow to reap rather than staying at home and hoping that God would send someone to bring the harvest to you. Most people want to serve a God that keeps manufacturing miracles daily. However, God knows that if we could only understand and exercise His principles, they will birth His miracles. His power would flow consistently into our lives. He wants us to build on His principles.

THE DIFFERENCE BETWEEN THE POOR AND THE RICH IS NOT IN WHAT THEY DO OR WHAT THEY HAVE BUT IN THE QUALITY OF THEIR HEARTS.

Remember, "You cannot travel within and standstill without. Your inside will always compel your outside to adjust. Yes, it takes time and it is hard work, but the principle works.

"Keep your heart with all diligence, for out of it spring the issues of life" [11]

This implies that it is hard work to change your mindset. It is painful but it is also gainful. The way rich people feel is different from the way poor people feel. When you mention money, the poor man sighs, but the rich man smiles. Poor people experience emotions like fear, frustration, anxiety, worry, discouragement, and rejection.

Imagine that someone sends a large amount of money to a church and says that each person in the church should be given a check of one million dollars on a particular Sunday. Then you receive your check for $1m, which you know could never bounce, and you leave for home looking sad and depressed. People ask you what happened and you tell them you are sad because you got a $1m check gift. Will your sadness make sense?

The real gist here is that the person who is hungry and cannot afford a plate of food cannot be feeling the same way as the person who is riding in a brand new Mercedes car, who can afford to eat anything he wants at anytime. The problem is that the average person does not understand how spiritual principles work. Most people allow circumstances to dictate their feelings. They do not realize that your feelings can affect your circumstances.

"All the days of the afflicted are evil, but he who is of a merry heart has a continual feast."[12]

If you want to be feasting financially everyday, you should have a merry heart. I will paraphrase that verse this way: "It is not because things are bad that you are sad, it is because you are sad that things are bad." Get out of depression, grief, sorrow and sadness. These emotions drive miracles away from your life.

"Because you did not serve the Lord your God with joy and gladness of heart, for the abundance of all things, therefore, you shall serve your enemies, whom the Lord will send against you, in hunger, in thirst, in nakedness, and in need of all things; and He will put a yoke of iron on your neck until He has destroyed you." [13]

This is an indication of poverty and it is all because the people addressed in the passage would not serve God with gladness and joy. That is why Nehemiah 8: 10 says: "The joy of the Lord is your strength." Whatever takes away your joy has taken away your prosperity. Money flows in the direction of energy. It is difficult to succeed in life in an area that you are not enthusiastic about. The sales men who sell the best are the ones who are excited about what they are selling.

You must feel rich before you become rich. Yes, you may be broke, but the spiritual principle requires that you feel like someone who is not broke for things to change.

CHANGE YOUR VISION

Your visions and dreams, the pictures you see with your inner eye, must change because provision connotes vision. You cannot separate provision from vision. "Pro" means "for" or "towards;" so the material prosperity you have is what God provides for your vision. It is no surprise that He says:

"Where there is no vision, the people perish." [14]

Where is the big business that was not once a dream in someone's mind? Where is the wealthy nation whose wealth was not once a definite dream in some people's hearts? That is why people are poor when there is no vision. What is the size of your dream? What can you see with your inner eye? What do you see about your future concerning your marriage, your family, your business and the people around you? If you do not have time to dream, then you do not have the time to prepare for your future. The dreams of today are the realities of tomorrow.

THE DREAMS OF TODAY ARE THE REALITIES OF TOMORROW.

If you do not have dreams today, it means you do not have the raw materials that God can use to construct your tomorrow. You cannot do without a dream. There must be a picture playing in your mind. Your picture and your mind work like a film fixed in a camera. For God to bless you, He needs to be able to print out a good picture in alignment with His, from the film inside you. One of the reasons why people pray without getting answers is because the pictures in their hearts do not usually agree with their prayer points.

"Now to him who is able to do exceeding abundantly above all that we ask or think, according to the power that works in us."[15]

What you think weighs as much as what you say in prayer. God also said to Abraham:

"Lift up your eyes now and look from the place where you are-northward, southward, eastward, and westward; for all the land which you see, I give to you and your descendants forever."[16]

It was Abraham that was required to see and not God. God already saw great things for Abraham. You have to see enough to leave for posterity. Stop making small plans because you serve a big God. Abraham had to see for himself and his children. It is said that a former French Prime Minister made this statement: "Make big plans. Don't make small plans. Big plans attract big people. Small plans attract small people and small people cause big problems."

There are people God has stationed around your life to assist you to fulfill your dreams one way or the other, but until you start dreaming of doing and attempting the things that will require their assistance, they may not bless you. They are the new wine God will inject into your life when you become the new wineskin. There are people who have the money you need to start your business, and people who have the job of your dream. Some control the contracts still beyond your reach. Until you start attempting things that will move you into their realms and create a need for their resources, they will not come. Dream big. Dream wild. Have a big vision inside of you.

"I will stand my watch and set myself on the rampart, and watch to see what He will say to me, and what I will answer when I am corrected. Then the Lord answered me and said; "Write the vision and make it plain on tablets, that he may run who reads it."[17]

Whatever you have to do to get a dream from God, do it. There is a difference between the dream God gives you and the one you cook up for yourself. God gives people dreams, visions, impressions or ideas for their future. In fact, if you are baptized in the Holy Spirit and speak in tongues, one of the major assignments of the Holy Spirit is to give you visions and dreams. That is the way He communicates with you.

"But this is what was spoken by the prophet Joel; And it shall come to pass in the last days, says God, that I will pour out of My Spirit on all flesh; your sons and your daughters shall prophesy, your young men shall see visions, your old men shall dream dreams."[18]

To prophesy means to hear from God and to say what you are hearing. You ought to be hearing from heaven.

I was a young man going nowhere; living by chance and hoping that some day, God might favor me. But when I received Christ and got filled with the Holy Spirit, I began to see things about my future in my mind. I began to feel that I was going to live a life of significance and touch a lot of people's lives. When I prayed, I would see myself preaching, though I was an Engineering student. That is what the Holy Spirit does to you. He gives you dreams, because that is the only way to alter your future and give you a better destiny. Paul prayed for the Ephesian Christians that God should give them the spirit of wisdom and knowledge of Him. In verse 18, he said:

"The eyes of your understanding being enlightened, that you may know what is the hope of His calling and what are the riches of the glory of His inheritance in the saints."[19]

He was talking about the Holy Spirit coming upon you and opening your inner eyes to see God's design for your destiny. That was how I could see myself preaching. You will begin to see the powerful provision God has made for believers. The key phrase in verse 18 is 'the riches,' not the poverty of the saints. There is wealth and blessing provided for you as a child of God.

My challenge to you as a child of God is to begin to see.

A DREAM IS THE ONLY WAY TO
ALTER YOUR FUTURE
AND TO GIVE YOU A BETTER
DESTINY WITH YOUR
INNER EYES. STEP INTO A NEW
LEVEL OF FINANCES.

Learn to dream. In spite of the natural circumstances outside, see something different inside.

Your outside must always catch up with your inside. So when I was barely finding enough to eat, I was eating delicious delicacies inside. The Holy Spirit taught me to dream. So in my dreams, I was in five-star hotels eating different varieties of excellent meals. I wore second-hand clothes when our family business went down, but I wore them only on my outside. On my inside, I was wearing clothes with designer labels. I did not have a choice. If I wanted to have a better future I had to get to know designer names like Hugo Boss, Giorgio Armani, Pacchioti, and so on.

If you do not want to be broke in old age, you have to start from now. You have to see it. What you see inside you today is what you will see on the outside tomorrow. Provision follows vision.

In Habakkuk 2, the prophet insisted he would stay on his watch until God said something. In some areas of my life, I have had to pray and meditate for some weeks before I got an answer and a picture in my spirit. The good thing is when God speaks, miracles begin. Your destiny begins to manifest. So I will advice you to stay in His presence until you hear Him. Stop expecting God to perform some magic for you. He wants to do something beyond magic. He wants to work miracles for you, but these miracles come by practicing His principles. If you pursue His principles, then you will be able to produce the miracles on a daily and consistent basis.

"He made known His ways to Moses and His acts to the children of Israel."[20]

His acts are the miracles, but His ways are the principles. The children of Israel just wanted the miracles and whenever the miracles stopped or they had problems, they murmured against Moses. But Moses knew the principles. You too will lead in this generation. Information is the key to transformation. Develop a new vision and a new dream through prayer, meditation and associating with rich people.

ACTION PLAN

The major difference between the rich and the poor is internal. Being rich is a matter of the heart. Albert Einstein is reputed to have famously said: "For us to do things the way we have always done them, and to expect different results is one of the definitions of insanity."

If you keep doing the same things while expecting different results, you are simply going around in circles. To be rich, you must change your thinking, your emotions, your vision, your confessions and your actions.

Let us find out how you can change your attitude and develop a wealth mentality.

1. How do you measure your self-worth? Is it by who you are or what you have?

....

....

2. Which is better: to be rich or to be poor? Why?

....

....

3. Is it true that money is the root of all evil?

....

4. Who are the people who advise you about your finances?

....

....

....

5. What is your reaction to successful and rich people? How do you perceive them?

....

....

6. How do you react to seemingly impossible breakthrough ideas?

....

....

PONDER OVER THE FOLLOWING

You can never be poor if you:

* Support your thinking with the Bible
* Read the books rich people write
* Associate with rich people
* Are careful about those who advise you.
* Make your money work for you

7. It takes money to make money. Yes or No?

8. How many books do you have on finances?
(a) Less than 5 (b) 5-10 (c) 11-20
(d) 21-30 (e) 31-40 (f) more than 40

9. List five negative emotions?

....

....

....

....

....

10. List five positive emotions?

....

....

....

....

....

11. How can you change your emotions from negative to positive?

....

....

12. What is your vision for your life?

....

....

13. How does it affect your thinking?

....

....

14. If you do not have a vision, come up with one now and explain why.

....

....

....

15. How do you refer to yourself: a rich or a poor person?

....

16. Have you been behaving like a rich person?

....

CHAPTER
3
FINANCIAL INTELLIGENCE

"The rich rules over the poor, And the borrower is servant to the lender."[1]

You are not really free until you are economically free. If you exclude finances from the blessings of God, you are in danger of being enslaved, because the rich rules over the poor. You need to prosper in order to exert the required measure of influence on the world. So get ready for financial breakthroughs. You must be prepared. As we have already discussed, the major area you have to address is your thinking. Thoughts are powerful. Make thinking big your starting point.

Everything on the face of the earth started from an intangible state of thoughts, ideas and dreams. If things are not happening in your thinking, then they are not happening in your life. Let us start thinking practically for financial breakthroughs.

Napoleon Hill, from his interviews with hundreds of successful people, enumerated six steps to aid accurate thinking for success.

IF THINGS
ARE NOT
AFFECTING
YOUR
THINKING,
THEN THEY
ARE NOT
AFFECTING
YOUR LIFE.

1. Decide on a definite goal.

When you plan money acquisition, do not think in vague terms. Decide on specific amounts of money. Nothing becomes dynamic until it becomes specific. You would not make any progress from where you are until you become very specific about what you want.

2. Decide on a definite time frame. Give it a deadline.
3. Write down your goals.
4. Develop a plan to achieve your goals.
5. Decide what you are ready to give in return. Know the price you are ready to pay.
6. Think about your goals everyday.

The keyword here is planning. Don't just talk about making money without planning. Planning implies strategic thinking. Jesus described this in Luke 14: 28-31 where He gave two illustrations that had to do with planning.

"For which of you, intending to build a tower, does not sit down first and count the cost, whether he has enough to finish it, lest, after he has laid the foundation, and is not able to finish, all who see it begin to mock him, saying, 'This man began to build and was not able to finish.' Or what king, going to make war against another king, does not sit down first and consider whether he is able with ten thousand to meet him who comes against him with twenty thousand? Or else, while the other is still a great way off, he sends a delegation and asks conditions of peace."[2]

These two illustrations refer to planning. Counting the cost is planning. No good house is built without a plan. Architects spend between five and seven years in school to study the planning and construction of buildings. In essence, Jesus was saying that you have to finish the house in your thoughts and on paper before you even begin the physical construction. It is the same with warfare and even finances.

For a long time, all I heard in church about warfare was about binding the devil and sweating it out while praying. But Jesus said you should also sit down and think. If you do not win on paper, you would not win on the battleground. A good chunk of our spiritual warfare incentives in the church is wasted because it leaves out accurate thinking. This is unlike God who is not an erratic person that detests thinking. He said:

"Come now, and let us reason together, …though your sins are like scarlet, they shall be as white as snow…"[3]

God wants to reason with you so that your life can be better. The way a 21-year-old son and a four-year-old child relate to their father should be different. Hence, God expects spiritual adults to sit down and plan under His guidance. If you continue to think the way the majority think, then you cannot achieve better results. We have to learn to call the shots in the economic system. God spoke to Moses and said:

DON'T JUST TALK ABOUT MAKING MONEY WITHOUT PLANNING. PLANNING IMPLIES STRATEGIC THINKING.

"And let them make Me a sanctuary, that I may dwell among them. According to all that I show you, that is, the pattern of the tabernacle and the pattern of all its furnishings, just so you shall make it."[4]

This passage infers that God likes to plan.

"Then the Lord answered me and said: "Write the vision and make it plain on tablets, that he may run who reads it."[5]

Without vision, there is no provision. Strategic thinking is the act of making vision plain on tablets. Most of the time, the vision God shows you is the picture of the end. So, you need to calculate from where you are to the end point that God showed you. If you cannot locate how you will get there in your mind, you may get lost in between.

Planning was Joseph's major asset in the Bible (Genesis 41). Interpreting Pharaoh's dream was not Joseph's only key to breakthrough. Interpreting Pharaoh's dream was just the identification of the problem. It brought him out of prison but did not secure him the seat of Prime Minister. Joseph went further by proffering the solution.

Pharaoh had dreamt about the seven years of famine, so what next? That was where Joseph's skills, training, development and preparation came in. He had learnt how to strategize. That was why he was prospering in Potiphar's house. That was why they also had to put everything in his hands in prison. Joseph had superior management ability. It was thus easy for him to suggest the plan to get out of famine. He suggested a plan of saving twenty percent in the time of plenty and building storehouses and warehouses in the city so that they would survive the years of famine.

The world goes around in cycles. The dream Pharaoh saw was not just for Egypt. The years of plenty and famine apply to everybody. The wise one who plans ahead will always master and dominate famine. When other countries were going poor and broke, Egypt was exploding in wealth. With accurate planning you can be on top, even twenty to thirty years from now. At the time when your contemporaries are broke, if you plan ahead, with the help of the Holy Spirit, you will be on top.

I observed that in the time of plenty, Egypt saved twenty percent for seven years, and when the years of famine came, there was abundance to the extent that they could sell to other countries. The issue here is that the law of compound interest increased the value of their savings.

Let us define some practical steps that you can apply to your life.

THE YEARS OF PLENTY AND FAMINE APPLY TO EVERYBODY. THE WISE ONE WHO PLANS AHEAD WILL ALWAYS MASTER AND DOMINATE FAMINE

1. Decide what your expenses will be at your retirement age.

That is the age you hope to achieve financial freedom. Financial freedom means that you have gotten to a stage where your expenses will be met even when you have stopped working. Some people put this age at forty-five. It could be thirty. Try and estimate how much you will need to spend at that age. I have discovered from studies that most millionaires had plans like this. I also discovered that the earlier people plan their lives, the higher they rise in their careers. This is referred to as the law of time perspective. If you would not be broke at sixty, it is almost too late to start planning at fifty-five.

2. Determine how much you need to have in investments to yield that amount at a realistic interest rate.

If you have decided to spend a particular amount at age sixty, what you will need to meet those expenses could be the interest on the money you have in a fixed-term certificate of deposit. Being rich means the dividends from your investment can meet your expenses. In a poor community, people easily believe that the person on salaried employment with a cute car is rich. However, if such people lose their jobs, they may be broke within six months. This category of people are not rich, they only have the potential to be rich if only they will plan with their resources.

3. Calculate how much you need to invest at a compounded interest rate to achieve the required amount.

God designed for things to increase in geometric progression and not arithmetically. He said we should multiply. That is why you get hundreds of corn from just one corn seed. When you work by the law of compound interest, you are making time to work for you. If you do not understand the law of compound interest, you will eat your harvest along with the potential seed that could have brought more multiplication over time. Eat the bread because God gives seed to the sower and bread to the eater. But, please do something worthwhile with your seeds.

Consider this simple example. If you save up $10,000 in a year and invest the funds at an interest of 12 per cent per annum, at the end of the year you get $11, 200. Time has worked for you and increased your money.

However, remember our law of time perspective: the longer the time, the more your multiplication in compound interest. So, it makes sense for you to start early in life. When you do calculations like this, you will realize you just may have been assuming that things were okay with your finances when they were not.

Let's work with some figures. $10,000 at 12 per cent compounded over 30 years yields $299, 599. Time has worked for you to turn your $10,000 into about $300,000. Let us assume that you increase your investment by adding $10,000 every year for the next 30 years at the same interest rate. It will yield $2,702,925. That means we can all become millionaires in 30 years if we invest $10,000 a year. I can assure you that by the time you have accumulated about $2.8 million, your financial advisor would definitely help you invest at a good interest rate. A further calculation based on investing this $2,702,925 at 15 per cent per annum yields $405,439 in a year. Note that this $405, 439 is just

EVERYTHING ON THE FACE OF THE EARTH STARTED FROM AN INTANGIBLE STATE OF THOUGHTS, IDEAS AND DREAMS.

your interest and the principal sum of $2,702,925 is still intact. If you decide to spend the interest, you get an average allowance of about $34,000 monthly.

When I did my own calculation and made provision for all my expenses, it was easy for me to conclude on how much I need to save and invest each year. However, you will recall that in the previous chapter, Jesus said putting your money in the bank is the least form of investment. It involves the lowest risks. In investing, the higher the risk, the higher the returns. These are my suggestions:

SAVE

Save from every pay check. It is also a matter of "pay now and play later" or "play now and pay later." Whichever one you choose, you will still need to pay sometime. It is either you experience the pain of discipline today or the pain of regret tomorrow. Save every increase in income. Do not blow your salary raises. Try not to adjust your standard of living immediately there is a raise in income. Save up the difference for sometime.

Save unexpected income. Usually, whenever unexpected income materializes, unexpected expenditures follow it. It is called Parkinson's Law. The law says that expenses will always rise to meet income. You must consciously fight this law. Solomon said, "When goods increase, they increase who eat them..."[6] This implies that when extra money comes into your hands, things that were not urgent before suddenly become urgent. Buying things that you were not even thinking about now seem like a do or die affair. Refuse to yield to this temptation. It is better for you to invest your money and secure a good future for yourself.

ACQUIRE SHARES

Don't leave your money idle in the bank. Banks make a lot of money from other people's money. The rate of inflation, particularly in poor economies, can make you lose money in real terms when it is higher than the bank's interest rate. Invest in fixed term certificates of deposits, shares of companies or real estate. When you invest in shares, you become part owner of a company and make other people work for you.

You can invest in some companies to exercise influence and to have a voice in their affairs. In my country, a Christian group bought shares in a tobacco company and forced the company to put the notice: "Tobacco Smoking Is Dangerous To Your Health" on its packs. This notice has since become a law for all tobacco companies in the country. When you have money, you have a voice. If you have enough shares in a company, you can become a director or even the chairman. Also, at the company's year-end, you stand to gain dividends and sometimes bonus shares from your investment in the company.

I will however advise you to talk to experts. Don't use only what you read on the pages of newspapers to determine your investment decisions. Use the services of stockbrokers or financial advisers with a good track record. To get the best out of shares, do it long term. You may speculate for some time so that you can build up your funds, but have a long-term focus. In addition, as a believer, always listen to the Holy Spirit in your decision-making.

At a seminar organized by a club in Nigeria, an illustration was given where someone in 1990, used 5,000 Naira (the Nigerian currency) to buy 10,000 units of shares at N0.5 each. With each passing year, the man was being given bonus shares. In 1995, he used N125, 000 to buy another 25,000 shares at N5 each. The man spent N130, 000 in all. By 1998, he had accumulated 174,500 shares and the value of the shares had increased. His initial investment of 1990 had multiplied to N5, 235,000 by 1998.

These are the secrets that rich people know which give them advantage over many others. There are elderly people today who read the report of the stock exchange daily because they thrive on dividends and bonus shares. Investing in shares is better than merely saving in banks.

This information is particularly important in parts of the world where governments are privatizing state-owned corporations. In a developing economy, shares appreciate a lot. When the privatization exercise starts, shares would be sold at very low prices. It is best for you to buy when the price is low and watch the values soar.

BE AN ENTREPRENEUR

Another level of investment is entrepreneurship. You can start your business. Make or sell something. It is not difficult to start a small business. Choose to not be fearful. There are many green areas waiting to be exploited. The problem is that we tend to see problems instead of opportunities. Set out to meet people's needs. Even in church ministry, there are many green areas not being exploited. Even in areas where there are champions, there is still plenty of room for competition. It is the ground that is crowded; there is enough room at the top for you and me.

In business, you have to cater for enough people. Some believe what they need is a building, but this is not so. Your primary need is customers. People want what you have to sell, not just the location you sell it at. Be ready to overcome rejection and failure. This is a common issue in business. Due to the level of development in some countries, entrepreneurial thinking is not yet developed; so when you take a bold step at business, people think you are over-reaching your limits, and expect you to fail. Do not listen to cynics. Success can grow out of failure. If things don't work out, you have not failed. You have just learnt how things would not work. Don't internalize your failure. It is just an event.

*IF THINGS DO NOT WORK OUT,
YOU HAVE NOT FAILED. YOU HAVE JUST
LEARNT HOW THINGS WOULD NOT WORK.
DO NOT INTERNALIZE YOUR FAILURE,
IT IS JUST AN EVENT.*

The most successful salesmen have suffered a lot of rejection. If you want to be a professional soccer player, you cannot insist that you must score a goal every time you play soccer. Get out and do what you must do, and be consistent.

When I started out in ministry, there were people I talked to who made me feel like I made a mistake. Of course I did not stay around such people. Each time you record a failure, encourage yourself like David did. Don't let the fear of failure keep you in poverty. There is plenty of money moving around you. Don't let fear keep you from getting it.

You must be persistent. Learn from your mistakes and move on. Always improve on the quality of your service or product. Be ready to add value to people's lives in whatever area of specialty you are in. Invest in your earning ability. Check today how much you can earn with the level of skill you have developed. Improve on it if it falls short of getting you to the position where you believe you will be comfortable enough to live, save and invest. It is worth it to take from your savings to invest in your earning ability.

"A wise man will hear and increase learning."[7]

Increasing learning is increasing expertise. There is a connection between learning and earning. What you learn affects what you earn.
"Do you see a man who excels in his work, he will stand before kings and not stand before unknown men." [8]

Mere men cannot afford to pay you what kings would pay. Skills give you capacity to solve problems. You should prepare to solve problems at high levels.

"If the axe is dull, and it's edge unsharpened, more strength is needed but skill will bring success."[9]

The acquisition of skill is important. For a long time, some church people thought that they could manipulate God into giving them powerful breakthroughs by only praying and fasting. They did not factor in adding value or meeting needs. It does not work that way. Skill is also important. Prayer and fasting are necessary but they cannot take the place of skill. If your job has to do with speaking, learn how to speak well. I will not part with my money if you cannot communicate intelligently.

If we do not acquire the highest level of skills we are capable of, we are just role models in words only. If you have identified your gifting, shoot to be part of the top five per cent in your area of calling in your nation over time. The essence of ministry for all Christians is not for everyone to become a pastor.

Ministry means you should shine the light in whatever area you are through service. Be the best doctor if you are a doctor, so that other doctors can listen to you. When you have excellent results in your field, people will listen to you.

A good number of the authors of books in the Bible were involved in secular pursuits. Daniel was a bureaucrat. He saw visions to solve national problems. David was not a pastor in a church office; he was a government ruler. Abraham was a farmer and the founding father of a nation. Be an expert in your field.

If you are promoted beyond your wisdom or skill, there will be a big problem. That is why God is waiting on you to improve your skills before bringing your financial break-through, so that you can manage the opportunities and resources well. It is your turn to become wealthy.

WHEN YOU HAVE EXCELLENT
RESULTS IN YOUR FIELD,
PEOPLE WILL LISTEN TO YOU.

ACTION PLAN

You are not really free until you are economically free. If you exclude finances from the blessings of God then you are enslaved because the rich rules over the poor.

1. Do you often think there is abundance in your nation or do you think there is lack?

....

2. Five steps to help accurate thinking for success.

a. Decide on a definite goal.

b. Decide on a definite time frame

c. Decide what you are ready to give in return

d. Think about your goal everyday

e. Write down your goals

3. The key word here is planning.

a) Write down 10 goals you plan to accomplish in your lifetime.

....
....
....
....
....
....
....
....
....
....

b) Write down 10 goals you plan to achieve in the next 10 years.

....
....
....
....
....
....
....
....
....
....

c) Write down 10 goals you plan to achieve in the next one year.

....
....
....
....
....
....
....
....
....
....

ONE-YEAR TURN-AROUND

d) Write down your targeted monthly income this time next year

....

e) Write a specific date for its accomplishment next year.

....

f) State the work, product or service you will offer in return for that income.

....
....
....

4. Journey To Financial Freedom

a) Decide your retirement age, that is, the age at which the income from your investments can pay your bill if you do not work another day in your life.

....

b) Estimate what your monthly expenses will be at that age.

....

c) Determine how much you need to have in investments at a realistic interest rate to yield what will pay your bills.

....

Example:

If your estimated expenses at age 60 is $20,000 per month, which comes to $240,000 per year. If you get 10 per cent interest per year on your investment, $240,000 is 10 per cent of $2.4 million. Therefore, you need to have $2.4 million in investments at the age of 60 years.

d) Calculate how much you need to invest yearly with compound interest to achieve the required investment figure at your retirement age. (See Tables 3.1-3.3)

....

Example:

If you are 30 years old, you have another 30 years to build your investment to $2.4 million. Assume you will earn 10 per cent interest yearly on your investments.

According to Table 3.1, assuming 10 per cent compound interest, you will build $1,200,000 in 30 years if you save $16 daily.

To build $2.4 million in 30 years, you must save $32 daily. That means, you must save $32 X 30 = $960 a month. Go through the steps and come up with your own figures.

5. Practical Steps

a) Save from every paycheck
b) Save unexpected income
c) Invest in a Fixed Term Certificate of Deposit
d) Invest in shares of profitable companies
e) Invest in start-up companies
f) Invest in real estate
g) Start your own business (this has a high rate of returns)
6. Increase your earning abilities. What you learn determines what you earn.

What do you need to do in the next one year to improve your skills?

....

....

....

....

TABLE 3.1

(Figures are in thousands of dollars)
At 5 per cent interest annually

* **DS** = Daily Savings

DS*	5yrs	1Oyrs	15yrs	20yrs	30yrs	41yrs	45yrs	54yrs
$1	2	5	8	13	25	50	60	100
$2	4	10	16	26	50	100	120	200
$3	6	15	24	39	75	150	180	300
$4	8	20	32	52	100	200	240	400
$5	10	25	40	65	125	250	300	500
$6	12	30	48	78	150	300	360	600
$7	14	35	56	91	175	350	420	700
$8	16	40	64	104	200	400	480	800
$9	18	45	72	117	225	450	540	900
$1O	20	50	80	130	250	500	600	1000
$11	22	55	88	143	275	550	660	1100
$12	24	60	96	156	300	600	720	1200
$13	26	65	104	169	325	650	780	1300
$14	28	70	112	182	350	700	840	1400
$15	30	75	120	195	375	750	900	1500
$16	32	80	128	208	400	800	960	1600
$17	34	85	136	221	425	850	1020	1700
$18	36	90	144	234	450	900	L080	1800
$19	38	95	152	247	475	950	1140	1900
$20	40	100	160	260	500	1000	1200	2000

TABLE 3.2
(Figures are in thousands of Dollars)

* **DS** = Daily Savings

DS*	5yrs	10yrs	15yrs	20yrs	30yrs	41yrs	45yrs	54yrs
$1	3	6	13	25	75	200	300	1000
$2	5	12	25	50	150	400	600	2000
$3	8	18	38	75	225	600	900	3000
$4	10	24	50	100	300	800	1200	4000
$5	13	30	63	125	375	1000	1500	5000
$6	15	36	75	150	450	1200	1800	6000
$7	18	42	88	175	525	1400	2100	7000
$8	20	48	100	200	600	1600	2400	8000
$9	23	54	113	225	675	1800	2700	9000
$10	25	60	125	250	750	2000	3000	1000
$11	28	66	138	275	825	2200	3300	11000
$12	30	72	150	300	900	2400	3600	12000
$13	33	78	163	325	975	2600	3900	13000
$14	35	81	175	350	1050	2800	4200	14000
$15	38	90	188	375	1125	3000	4500	15000
$16	40	96	200	400	1200	3200	4800	16000
$17	43	102	213	425	1275	3400	5100	17000
$18	45	108	225	450	1350	3600	5400	18000
$19	48	114	238	475	1425	3800	5700	19000
$20	50	120	250	500	1500	4000	6000	20000

At 10% Interest annually

TABLE 3.3
(Figures are in thousands of Dollars)

* **DS** = Daily Savings

At 15% Interest annually

DS*	5yrs	10yrs	15yrs	20yrs	30yrs	41yrs	45yrs	54yrs
$1	3	10	20	50	100	250	1000	5000
$2	5	20	40	100	200	500	2000	10000
$3	8	30	60	150	300	750	3000	15000
$4	10	40	80	200	400	1000	4000	20000
$5	13	50	100	250	500	1250	5000	25000
$6	15	60	120	300	600	1500	6000	30000
$7	18	70	140	350	700	1750	7000	35000
$8	20	80	160	400	800	2000	8000	40000
$9	23	90	180	450	900	2250	9000	45000
$10	25	100	200	500	1000	2500	10000	50000
$11	28	110	220	550	1100	2750	11000	55000
$12	30	120	240	600	1200	3000	12000	60000
$13	33	130	260	650	1300	3250	13000	65000
$14	35	140	280	700	1400	3500	14000	70000
$15	38	150	300	750	1500	3750	15000	75000
$16	40	160	320	800	1600	4000	16000	80000
$17	43	170	340	850	1700	4250	17000	85000
$18	45	180	360	900	1800	4500	18000	90000
$19	48	190	380	950	1900	4750	19000	95000
$20	50	200	400	1000	2000	5000	20000	100000

CHAPTER
4
FINANCIAL MANAGEMENT

"There is desirable treasure, and oil in the dwelling of the wise, but a foolish man squanders it all."[1]

To be financially successful, you must learn to spend less than you earn. You have to learn to save. The starting point on your journey to financial prosperity is for you to cross the line from foolishness to wisdom by controlling your appetite. We have talked about Parkinson's Law, which states that expenses will always rise to meet income. You must fight Parkinson's Law. Learn to save. It is a scriptural principle. In the world's financial system, you are advised to save at least ten per cent of your income.

Joseph advised Pharaoh to save at least twenty per cent of the produce for every year during the years of surplus. When you have cultivated the habit of saving, learn to invest, and let the law of compound interest work for you over a long period of time.

It is also important that you consistently increase your earning ability. If you set goals and you have a strong desire, God will give you the ability to develop better skills. Your earning power should not remain the same year in, year out. You should increase over the years because the path of the just is like the shining light that shines more and more until the perfect day. Your income should increase every year, as well as your investments.

"A prudent man foresees evil and hides himself. The simple pass on and are punished."[2]

You need to stay clear of certain people and advices. Get advice from experts and people who have personal results. I am sharing these things because I have a burden. Where there is a spiritual shift and revival, they should be followed by economic revival and technological breakthroughs. The industrial revolution was preceded by revival. What is happening in some parts of the world is not happenstance. The move of God will be followed by economic empowerment.

God did not deliver Israel from slavery in Egypt without giving them money to take along. We should not expect anything less. That is why we are preparing ourselves to create and manage wealth.

GET-RICH-QUICK SCHEMES

If you want to get rich quickly, you are on your way to poverty at a fast pace. I advocate making long-term plans because there is no amount of heat that can cause a block of ice to melt instantly. The law of time perspective says that the longer the time you take into reckoning while making your decisions and taking actions, the higher you will rise on the ladder of financial success. If you want to become rich quickly, you will get your fingers burnt.

Unfortunately, the more people suffer, it seems as though the more desperate and stupid they become. Otherwise, all the tricksters would be out of business. If you are not saved and you do not have the Spirit of God to give you contentment, you will be covetous;

which will make it easy for some trickster with a get- rich-quick scheme out there to get you. Don't allow your money to fall into the hands of tricksters and schemers. Wealth building is a long-term process.

To be a smart investor, note that the higher the risk you take, the more money you will make. If you want to get the best returns from companies, you could invest in new companies in whose management you trust. New companies yield terrific returns because the managers of such companies are usually passionate and the rate at which their income multiplies is often faster. However, it is riskier than investing in established companies because it takes a lot to stabilize a company. Be led by the Spirit. Take time to pray and then make a decision.

IF YOU WANT TO GET RICH QUICKLY, YOU ARE ON YOUR WAY TO POVERTY AT A FAST PACE.

INVESTING IN REAL ESTATE

Another area I encourage you to invest in is real estate. Landed property will always appreciate except there is an unusual depression in the economy. Property appreciates along with inflation because landlords must pass their expenses down to tenants or to those who want to buy property. The rate of appreciation of property is usually phenomenal. Look for what you can afford for now, it will appreciate over time. Some areas that are on the outskirts of your city today will be right in the midst of the city some thirty years from now.

A pilot explained to me that he was compelled to buy a piece of land by his friend, who had bought some plots in the same area. He initially made a down payment to the owner. The first time he wanted to take someone to the site, he lost his way because the area was still largely in the woods. He had the opportunity of paying in installments and did not even realize when he had paid it off, until the landowner told him he had completed the payments. He told me this story twenty-three years after that purchase. He had built a house on it, that part of the city was now densely populated, and the property had appreciated so much in value.

Conquer the fear of lack. It is not as difficult as it seems to invest. Moreover, the fact that we are believers assures us of God's direction and favor.

THREE OPTIONS FOR INCREASE

CONQUER THE FEAR OF LACK. IT IS NOT AS DIFFICULT AS IT SEEMS TO INVEST.

Having encouraged you to increase your earning ability, consider prayerfully one of the following steps:

1. Rise to the top of the corporate ladder in your field.

Ask God whether He wants you to stay on a salaried job. The highest pay is usually at the top. Some years back, the CEO of a multinational company told me how he had joined the company and decided from start that he was going to become the CEO one day. Exactly fifteen years later, he became the CEO. You may rise to the point where you become a junior partner in a company but you need to have that as your vision from the start. Provision follows vision. If there is no way for you to rise to the top on your current job, pray and change jobs.

2. You could decide to rise to a certain level and then launch out on your own.

You need to acquire experience and expertise in your field so that when you launch out you will draw on the skills you have acquired.

3. Start your business.

We have discussed the benefits of savings and investment in stocks. However, entrepreneurship will pay you the most if you are cut out for it. If you offer products or services on your own, you will get the highest returns.

Instead of buying shares from other people's companies, being an entrepreneur makes you the one who owns the company that owns the shares. Instead of being a banker, you can own the bank.

If you want to start your own business, let me encourage you to conquer your fear. You cannot escape taking exceptional risks if you must succeed exceptionally. The greatest risk in this life is to take no risk. You must not be afraid of change even though it may threaten your life. Do what you have to do to get what you have to get.

Choose freedom over security: There is no security in security. Some people want to play it safe and all they are praying for is that they should never be laid off. That does not give a feeling of safety at all. If God does not want you to stay on a job, conquer your fear, and go for your dream. Walk by faith and not by sight. Things will not always

YOU CAN NOT ESCAPE TAKING EXCEPTIONAL RISKS IF YOU MUST SUCCEED EXCEPTIONALLY.

remain the way they are. Things will definitely change and the best way to manage change is not to wait for it, but to initiate it.

Obey the Spirit of God and start with what you have. Most people believe that what they need to start is something they do not have. Whatever it is you have is enough to start with. Get my book titled 'Start With What You Have' to get some ideas. Several people have started businesses with little, and now they are the better for it. A first year university student began to sell some things after reading one of our books. He testified that he no longer needed to depend on anyone for sustenance.

Your spiritual, mental and physical abilities are your greatest capital. Don't say you don't have anything to start with, especially if you can think. I heard someone say many years ago that there are three kinds of commerce.

1. Commerce by war: You overrun a country, kill everyone and take all the goods away.

2. Commerce by barter: You bring what you have, I bring what I have, and we exchange.

3. Commerce by creativity: You chunk out ideas to create or improve products, services and processes.

The wealthiest people in the world today are people who thrive on ideas.

"I will pour out my spirit upon all flesh, your sons and daughters shall prophesy, your young men shall see visions, your old men shall dream dreams."[3]

YOUR SPIRITUAL, MENTAL AND PHYSICAL ABILITIES ARE YOUR GREATEST CAPITAL.

You should not be short of divinely inspired ideas. We all know that ideas rule the world. We are now in the information age. As a Christian, you have access to creativity. Your mental ability is there. Above all, if it comes down to it, there is something you can do with your physical hands that would bring in some money to sustain you for today before you get your ideas together. Whichever way it goes, start with what you have.

Incorporate yourself and call your company "Me incorporated." You will immediately become the MD/CEO of this international company! When you do this, your mentality gives you a business perspective to everything you do, even when someone else hires you. It means "Me incorporated" is being hired by someone for a specific amount of money per month and when the company cannot afford your services anymore, you go somewhere else and offer your services.

Incorporate and market yourself. Package yourself the way you want to be bought. Keep on investing in your mental, physical and spiritual abilities. Improve yourself. You will never attract more value than you are worth. What you do not have the power to attract you do not have the power to retain. Life does not give you what you want; it gives you what you are. Ultimately, you will only attract what you are on the inside.

SUCCESS: INSPIRATION PLUS PERSPIRATION

Increase your capital base. Study, read and sharpen your technical expertise. For those who are starting out in business, remember Thomas Edison said, "Success is one per cent inspiration and ninety-nine per cent perspiration." This implies that all the lectures, counseling and reading you engage in only contribute one per cent to your success. The remaining 99 per cent takes place when you get out and do something about what you have been hearing and learning. You can be inspired and even fall under the anointing, but that is only one per cent of your success. Get out and sweat it out. There is no substitute for hard work in the school of success. It is not the hearer of the Word but the doer that is blessed.[4]

Smart work does not exclude hard work. Any smart work that does not have hard work in it is useless work. There is no prize without a price. You will realize this when you relate with rich and successful people. Hard work does not kill. It is stress and negative emotions that kill. Work hard, especially when you are just starting out in business.

BE PASSIONATE

You also need to be hungry. Have a strong desire, and develop a passion for your business. When you are just starting, you are at a disadvantage because some people started before you. So, you cannot be complacent. God does not grant wishes, He grants desires. You need to have a strong desire. Be hungry for success. It is that hunger that will help you overcome obstacles. It will prevent you from quitting easily. You will definitely meet challenges but you must not give up.

PRIORITIZE

Focus on what generates income. People start businesses and focus on things that will not yield a dime. The son of a wealthy man set up a business with the assistance of his grandfather. After about three months, his grandfather asked him how the business was doing. The man responded that he had equipped his office and hired employees but was not making any sales. The grandfather simply said; "Son, you do not need computers now, not even an office; all you need now is a lot of customers."

This goes for the person who is just starting out. Your primary needs are customers and a number of them already have people who are meeting their needs. So you need to beat your competition through good pricing and excellent quality.

ENJOY THE RIDE

Celebrate little successes. Break down your goals and record little successes. This will be of great encouragement to you. If you set only long-term goals, you may get discouraged and not realize that you have achieved a lot. Make daily goals and score yourself. Be like God who took six days to create the world. When He was through on the first day, He looked at what He had done and said it was good. Encourage yourself and celebrate little successes along the way.

Keep a very positive attitude. You may suffer disappointments, and instead of becoming better you become bitter. If you maintain a negative attitude, you will not get anywhere. Your attitude affects your altitude.

BUILD A SYSTEM

ENCOURAGE YOURSELF AND CELEBRATE LITTLE SUCCESSES ALONG THE WAY.

Build a system. Do not get bugged down with paper work as your business begins to grow. Know when to move to the next level and add new members of staff. This is the reason why many businesses fail. Ninety per cent of one-man businesses die in the first five years.

In ten years it increases to ninety-nine per cent. This is because the success of the business depends on only one person. So to increase income, the owner must work more. Eventually it affects other areas of the person's life. The person cannot go on vacation because the income of the whole company also goes on vacation.

Dream big from the start. Have the goal of building a system. A system is an entity where some parts operate as a whole to carry out a function. A person becomes ill when one or more of the systems in the body breaks down. There can be no growth if there is no health. When you run a healthy system, God will bring growth.

If you are a business person, you need to employ, train and develop people to the point where there will be people who can do things exactly the way you do them or even better. You have successfully built a system if in your absence the company continues to grow. Let your goal be a big one for your business. From the start, have a staff plan and get ready for a breakthrough.

HAVE A HEART THAT SUPPORTS GOD'S WORK. BE PASSIONATE FOR THE THINGS OF THE KINGDOM.

Don't ever lose focus and always remain a kingdom promoter. God gives one wealth so that one can bless and enhance His work here on earth. Have a heart that supports God's work. Be passionate for the things of the kingdom.

YOUR ACTION PLAN

Parkinson's Law states that expenses will always rise to meet income. You must fight Parkinson's Law. Learn to save. It is a profitable principle. In the world's financial system, you are advised to save at least ten per cent of your income.

1. If you have an opportunity to invest, what would you invest in?

....

2. What is the reason for your answer in number 1 above?

....

3. In your choice of investment, what would you prefer: freedom or security?

....

4. List 5 (five) business ideas you could invest in

....
....
....
....
....

5. Which of the above would be your best option?

....

6. Will your idea in question 5 generate income?
If yes, how? If no, why?

....
....

7. Would you prefer to become CEO in your current company or to start your our business?

....

8. If you meet with disappointment in your choice of investment, what would your attitude be?

....

9. List three steps you will take in the next 30 days to change your financial status?

....

....

....

If you achieve these, take time to celebrate and keep moving.

CHAPTER
5
MONEY
POWER

We are moving from the realms of financial manna to financial harvest. Much of what the body of Christ has focused on has been financial manna. When Israel was in the wilderness, they were not expected to work on any principle. They were not supposed to sow and reap anything. God brought the food everyday. But as soon as they stepped into the Promised Land, manna ceased because God did not design for us to live permanently on manna.

Manna comes through miracles. However, God wants us to step into the level where we understand His principles. We can take the seeds He gives us and cultivate them to get miracles and blessings that are more predictable.

God is delivering to us the principles that control the miracles. He wants the miracles in our lives to be consistent and ever increasing. Deprivation has put some people in a state of desperation for financial survival. Because of this, some are tempted to think only in the short-term. But if you are walking based on principles, you will make long-term plans.

"Come now, and let us reason together says the LORD. Though your sins are like scarlet, they shall be as white as snow. Though they are red as crimson they shall be as wool. If you are willing and obedient you shall eat the good of the land."[1]

The God that people like to talk about in some parts of the world is the God that is irrational and erratic: One that you have to beg to bless you once in a while. But the God of the Bible is highly predictable. That is why He gave us the Bible. And the interesting thing about God is that He thinks. Mental work is the real work. There is a dimension of blessing you do not get into until you have decided to reason with God.

YOUR UNIQUENESS AND WEALTH

Your financial abundance is tied to your passion for what you do. In other words, money flows in the direction of energy. You have got to identify those things that release your passion.

You should not be willing to do just anything. For example, I have no desire to treat sick people in the hospital. I do not dream of singing or playing the bass guitar. If I do these, I will be operating in the areas of my weakness. When you do not operate by grace, what you get is disgrace. In fact, the things I am not willing to do outnumber the things I am willing to do.

Your purpose in life dictates your passion. And I have come to discover that there is a powerful connection between your purpose and your money supply. Discover your personal purpose because that is the one thing that defines your passion, motivation and fulfillment.

I believe that one of the most powerful truths that will release your freedom is the truth about who you are. Discover who you are. You have got to build your life in line with your uniqueness. You have to know what your personal values and needs are. A man by the name, Don Harold said, "Unhappiness is not knowing what we want and killing ourselves to get it."

Definiteness of purpose is the most potent tool for wealth creation. God's power and anointing is locked inside divine purpose (Romans 8:28). Heaven's provision follows heaven's vision. If you develop a vision by yourself, then you have to find the provision by yourself.

DEFINITENESS OF PURPOSE IS THE MOST POTENT TOOL FOR WEALTH CREATION.

You must be absolutely sure of where you are going. Define what drives and motivates you because your financial breakthrough is tied to your uniqueness. It is very difficult for you to try to be somebody else and to get the same breakthroughs that the person is getting. It will be tough. You need to define your uniqueness.

Your purpose in life should affect the choice of your marriage partner, and your career. Understanding your assignment should dictate decisions in all the vital areas of your life. Your purpose is not your decision; it is your discovery. The questions you need to ask are; 'Who am I?" "Why am I here?" "Where am I coming from?" "Where am I going?" Find answers to these vital questions.

"I will stand my watch and set myself on the rampart, and watch to see what he will say to me and what I will answer when I am corrected."[2]

I suggest, first of all, that you discover your purpose. Identify your gifts and talents. Know your temperament. Discover your dominant traits. You have a combination of gifts that are unique to you. You cannot separate your financial breakthroughs from your gifts. You have to find out what you love and what you hate. And you need to pursue the things that make you different from others.

John Helmenson said; "Imitation is your limitation. The more you try to be like someone else, the less of yourself you become. And if you try to be like someone else, the best you can be is second best." God is not in the habit of producing duplicates. He is the God of originals. If someone you know is making financial progress and the person is an extrovert; you, an introvert cannot behave exactly like that person. You have to find what suits you.

Secondly, pray and ask God questions. We have to learn to ask God questions. There was a man in Acts16:30 who asked, "Sirs, what must I do to be saved?" You have got to ask the questions that will provoke quality answers. Prayer is absolutely necessary. It was in the place of prayer that God told me I was going to be a preacher.

QUALITY QUESTIONS PROMOTE QUALITY ANSWERS FROM GOD.

Thirdly, I am going to list a number of words and I want you to identify three that are most important to you because they define your values and your personal needs.

1. Adventure
2. Independence
3. Security
4. Family
5. Beauty
6. Love
7. Fun
8. Health
9. Happiness
10. Communication
11. Humor
12. Learning
13. Creativity
14. Respect ....
15. Emotional connection
16. Ministry ....

The list is actually longer than this, but what I am trying to do is to draw your attention to words that describe your personal values. Some people need adventures to thrive. This kind of people will be bored to death by routine. If they build their lives around jobs that are routine, they will kill themselves in the bid to earn a living. But for some others, fun is valuable.

Sometimes when you stay around people that are successful, they tend to expect you to succeed exactly the way they have succeeded. This can cause problems for you because your make up may be completely different from theirs. There are people who make money through entertainment. So if you are someone who loves fun and you want to start a business, a recreation club may be a good idea. Interestingly, you will be making your money while you are enjoying yourself. For some people, humor is it. It is not something they struggle to do. It is like they are specially wired for humor.

God has designed it that you would be blessed while you are doing what you enjoy doing. Some work for money and all they get from work is money. But those who have lined up their work with their personal values derive something more than money from their work. They derive fulfillment and self-worth because they operate in their area of expertise and gifting. Line up your life with your personal values and needs.

Some of us thrive on creativity. I tend to see better ways that things could be done. I love independence. I thrive better that way because I don't like to do things the conventional way. I love to experiment.

If you come around anyone that tries to make your gift or temperament seem inferior to his or hers, walk away from that person. You may never succeed around such a person. Nobody's gift is better than someone else's gift. We need all of the different gifts.

*GOD HAS DESIGNED IT THAT YOU
WOULD BE BLESSED WHILE YOU
ARE DOING WHAT YOU ENJOY DOING.*

George Bernard Shaw once said, "The reasonable man adapts himself to the world; the unreasonable man adapts the world to himself; therefore, all progress depends on the unreasonable man." Most people want to fit into the mould that has been designed by others. We tend to want to live up to other people's expectations. Learn not to fit into other people's schedules, but rather fit other people into your schedule. You only have one life to live.

That is what purpose does for you. It gives you a sense of direction. If you don't know where you are going, others will drag you to where they are going. If you do not have a vision of your own, you will spend your life fulfilling other people's visions. If you do not have a dream of your own, somebody will give you his or her own dreams to fulfill.

Learn to do things that suit you. I learned this when I began to relate with successful people. I found out they know what they want. They have strong values. It is not uncommon to see two highly successful people disagree because of their values. In such instances, both are likely to be right. Remember, successful people try to adapt the world to themselves.

IF YOU DO NOT HAVE A VISION OF YOUR OWN, YOU WILL SPEND YOUR LIFE FULFILLING OTHER PEOPLE'S VISIONS.

Every human being has a limited amount of resources that God has given him or her in life. You can expend those resources trying to please everybody. If you will be yourself, there is no way you would not incur the wrath of some people who expect you to be somebody else.

However, you already know that the best way to be blessed is for you to be yourself. You cannot satisfy everybody.

"For I say, through the grace given to me, to everyone who is among you, not to think of himself more highly than he ought to think, but to think soberly, as God has dealt to each one a measure of faith."[3]

Successful people do things with above average conviction and confidence. Find out the area where you know you cannot fail, your area of faith, and stay in it. Outside of that, you are a loser. There is an area of life where you stand before a crowd with confidence. Find it and function there.

There are certain things you do with confidence. Stay in those areas. Avoid the areas of life where you lose your confidence. There are certain indicators God has put inside of us that point us in the direction in which we are supposed to go. In Luke 4:32 when Jesus spoke, the Bible says His teaching astonished people because He spoke with authority.

SUCCESSFUL PEOPLE DO THINGS WITH ABOVE AVERAGE CONVICTION AND CONFIDENCE.

When you operate in that area of confidence, it is no longer natural faith that you are operating in but the faith that God has given to you. You will notice that you function with divine ability in that area. You may be timid in every other area but there is something that comes upon you when you stand in that area of confidence. A gift is a gift. A gift is like a precious stone in the eyes of him that has it, wherever it turns, it prospers.[4]

Develop confidence in your gift and build your life around it. There is no area of life where you cannot make your millions. You love cooking? There are millionaires who cook. You love baking? There are many millionaires who bake.

When the authorities asked Jesus to pay the temple tax, Jesus instructed Peter to go down to the river and to catch a fish. He said the money would be in the mouth of the fish.

The question here is, why ask Peter to catch a fish? Why not ask him to go catch a rabbit? It is because Peter loved fishing. Jesus literally pulled him from the fishing boat into the ministry. And when Jesus died and it seemed He was not going to resurrect on time, Peter announced to everybody, "I go fishing." You see, the day Jesus would provide money supernaturally, He told Peter to go fishing. When the anointing of the Spirit of God comes on your gift or that passion of yours, you will produce extraordinary results, especially with respect to your finances.

DEVELOP CONFIDENCE IN YOUR GIFT AND BUILD YOUR LIFE AROUND IT

Abraham was a livestock farmer and God blessed him through his livestock business. When Isaac came along, it should have been expected that he would inherit his father's profession but Isaac was into crop farming. That was his design. If you check out Cain and Abel, you will notice that Abel was a livestock farmer and Cain was into farm produce. Check out the difference between Esau and Jacob. Esau was a man who loved to go hunting in the bush but Jacob was someone who loved to stay around the house. Do what suits you. Stand out.

TURNING YOUR UNIQUENESS INTO MONEY

When you have defined your life work, purpose and values, identify moneymaking activities in line with them. Begin to think about the activities around your personal values that will bring money. There are activities in the area of your gifts that do not bring money. Treat those as hobbies.

Now that you have identified your own needs, it should be easier for you to meet other people's needs. Just spend your time meeting their needs. You can do it through quality service or quantity of sales. That is, you can either make money through quality by meeting the needs of an individual or make it through quantity by meeting the needs of a multitude. Either way, you cannot escape meeting other people's needs.

For example, a salesperson may make as much money as a doctor in a specific instance. The doctor treats just one person for a life threatening sickness, the salesperson sells to two hundred people and they make the same amount of money.

BE A PROBLEM SOLVER

That gift that God put inside you will solve a problem for someone. Joseph who was supposed to be a slave solved problems for Potiphar. When he landed in prison, he solved problems for the prison warder, and then solved problems for people who had dreams but did not understand the interpretation. Eventually, he made it to the palace solving

WHEN YOU HAVE DEFINED YOUR LIFE WORK, PURPOSE, AND VALUES, IDENTIFY MONEYMAKING ACTIVITIES IN LINE WITH THEM.

problems. That was the major key. David rose from obscurity to stardom in just one day in Israel because he solved a national problem. Money and promotion are rewards for the problems you solve.

CULTIVATE EXCELLENCE

Having discovered your purpose and gift, cultivate excellence.

"Do you see a man that is an expert in his craft; he shall stand before kings he shall not stand before ordinary men."[5]

Invest to increase your earning ability. You have got to develop expertise in some area. Get more training and education. Develop yourself. Aim to be one of the best in your profession. I do not believe that spirituality is synonymous with mediocrity. It grieves me when I see people in the church spend most of their time binding devils instead of developing their expertise. Sure, you should bind the devils, but you need to develop other skills. There is a level of expertise that will make you stand before kings. It is those kings that can afford to pay you the kind of money you want.

INVEST TO INCREASE YOUR EARNING ABILITY.

There is a kind of work you can do to earn the kind of money you are looking for. Take action. Nothing moves until you move. I did not develop my ability to teach the way I do today by accident. I have delivered thousands of sermons and lectures and each one is a rehearsal for the next one. Maximize the opportunities that you have at hand today. Do what you have to do to make progress. Do something with your gift. It may not bring you much money today, but success is not only about money.

NOTHING MOVES UNTIL YOU MOVE.

Develop your skills first. The best way to create opportunities for yourself is to bloom where you are planted.

ACTION PLAN

1. Definiteness of purpose is the most potent tool for wealth creation. State in one sentence your purpose in life.

....

....

2a. Identify from the list below the three that are most important to you because they define your values and personal needs.

a. Adventure
b. Independence
c. Security
d. Family
e. Beauty
f. Love
g. Fun
h. Health
i. Happiness
j. Communication
k. Humor
l. Learning
m. Creativity
n. Respect
o. Emotional connection
p. Ministry.

2b. List two moneymaking activities in each of those three areas of your choice?

....

....

Your financial abundance is tied to your passion about what you are doing to make money. In other words, money flows in the direction of energy.

3. What are those things that ignite your passion? List out six (6) of them.

....

....

....

....

....

....

4. Ask yourself some basic questions and answer them.

* Who am I?

....

....

* Why am I here?

....

....

* Where am I coming from?

....

....

* Where am I going?

....

....

5. Pray and ask God questions.

6. Start operating in your area of expertise and talents.

Learn not to fit into other people's schedules; rather fit other people into your schedule. You have only one life to live.

CHAPTER
6
THREE
RICH MEN

The importance of this message at this time cannot be over-emphasized. I believe that God wants us to have financial resources we can employ for the expansion of His kingdom. The church however was made to believe that God does not want us to be rich. This got to an extent that rich people felt uncomfortable in church.

Christians get on guilt trips when God begins to bless them. They get confused because they enjoy the things money does for them, yet they feel guilty for enjoying those same things. There are several biblical stories that seem to support the false doctrine that God wants His people to be poor. One of them can be found in Luke 16. Jesus told the story of a very wealthy man who died and went to hell while the beggar who sat his gate died and was carried to Abraham's bosom.

The false conclusion that was made from this passage is that rich people go to hell while poor people go to heaven. There is a misconception that poverty is synonymous with piety; that if you really suffer in this world, you will enjoy in heaven, but if you enjoy in this world you will suffer in hell. But Jesus never said such a thing. Why did the rich man go to hell? The rich man went to hell because he did not have a relationship with God and because of greed. If you read many of the stories that Jesus told about rich people, he showed very clearly that there is one big temptation that rich people face, and it is the temptation to give in to the spirit of greed.

"But those who desire to be rich fall into temptation and a snare and into many foolish and harmful lusts, which drown men in destruction and perdition. For the love of money is a root of all kinds of evil for which some have strayed from the faith in their greediness, and pierced themselves through with many sorrows."[1]

THE SPIRIT OF GREED

God is channeling money into your life but understand that any time money flows, the spirit of greed tries to accompany it attempting to use that same blessing that God has brought into your life to distort your view and perception of life.

When money comes into your life, it aims at taking only one place and it is the place that God has reserved for Himself. That was the main thing Jesus tried to address with rich people. The rich man in the story was clothed in purple. He was throwing parties daily. There was just one missing factor; what I call the G- factor. God was not part of his life, neither was God part of his wealth. God had no control over his wealth and the first proof is the way he treated the poor man.

The rich man was stingy; he gave nobody anything. He was throwing parties yet someone died of hunger right in front of his gate. If you listen to God in respect to your finances you will meet the needs of someone or a ministry around you. God will move you to give. God cannot stand to see people living in poverty, especially in the church.

The spirit of greed controlled this rich man. This is a big problem in some parts of the world. People will do anything to impress others to the extent that they will spend a lot of money on festivities, but refuse to be moved by God to give the same amount of money to someone who is suffering or for God's work. Some people will spend money they would not pay as tithes in the church on parties. This is greed.

In Mark 10, the Bible tells us that a very wealthy young man ran to Jesus, fell down at His feet and said, "Master, what must I do to inherit eternal life?" Jesus listed all the commandments in response and the young man said, "Master, I have kept all of those commandments from the time I was a young man." The Bible says;

"And Jesus loved him and told him, yet there is one thing that you lack, go your way, sell whatever you have and give to the poor and you will have treasure in heaven."[2]

Well, the young man walked away sorrowful because he was not willing to part with his great possessions. If you read between the lines you will see that it is not that he had great possessions; great possessions had him.

WHEN MONEY COMES INTO YOUR LIFE, IT AIMS AT TAKING ONLY ONE PLACE AND IT IS THE PLACE THAT GOD HAS RESERVED FOR HIMSELF.

Jesus loved him so much that he told him to sell everything that he had. The devil wants us to think that Jesus tries to make people he loves to become poor. But no, Jesus said that the young man lacked something. He saw the young man under the grip of greed and covetousness. He wanted to break the hold of greed over the young man's life. Money held the same position that God should have taken in the young man's life and Jesus wanted to break this hold.

As money begins to flow into your life in abundance, understand that the temptation to be greedy may accompany it. A number of people have been praying for a long time but have not increased financially because of greed. They've been failing God's covetousness test. In Genesis 22, God told Abraham, "Take your son, your only son whom you love, and go and offer him for me on mount Moriah."

This was his promised son; the hope and future of Abraham, who would carry Abraham's name. But God said I want him. But if you recall, when Abraham was about to sacrifice the young boy, God told him to hold it. It was just a test. Many are failing on the giving test. There is no amount of anointing oil that a pastor will pour on your head that will cause you to be blessed financially if you don't break free from greed by giving.

In Malachi 3:7-8 God says, "You have robbed me in tithes and offerings this whole nation and you are cursed with a curse." When you tithe, you pass the first stage of God's covetousness test. And that is where we play a whole lot of games on God. And God expects us to actually give ourselves to Him first.

You know what men did to protect themselves from losing money? They formed corporations. At a point in time there were no companies or corporations. You had your farm, which belonged solely to you. Your money was your money and your business was your company. But men invented corporations to protect their wealth and to avoid the payment of taxes.

For most rich people, it is their corporation that bears their personal expenses. It is the corporation that pays the children's school fees and pays for the first class flight tickets. Once the corporation pays for it, the money is not taxable because it is part of the corporation's expenses.

All of that will have to be deducted before the corporation calculates its profits and the remainder is taxed. That is the way it works in the world. But I want to encourage you if you are a Christian and God has helped you to establish a business, structure your corporation's finances in such a way that it gives also. Your company's money is your money, if you run a small business. I am saying this because the spirit of greed will want to make you hold back as much as you can.

Take Africa for example, the spirit of greed is at the root of the continent's problem; and it is because of its high level of poverty. Political offices have become one of the major avenues for financial breakthroughs for greedy individuals. Contending for political office then becomes a do-or-die affair. Once people get into political offices, they suddenly have access to the kind of money they have never handled before and greed steps in.

The problem with this kind of wealth is that it has a time limit. There is the spirit of greed that seeks to manipulate public office holders even when they mean well. At first they come in and expose all the atrocities of the previous administration, then after some time it becomes public knowledge that they are not different from that previous one. They begin to sit tight. Some have even made up their minds to die in office. It is the spirit of greed. Greed is terrible. The only disciple Jesus lost was not lost to adultery or fornication but to greed.

There is a temptation that money brings. It tries to transfer your trust from God to it. You see, when you do not have much, you may not have a choice but to trust God. But when the money starts flowing in, you have to be careful not to make it your source of self-esteem, such that when money is not there you sometimes feel inferior to other people. But, you must get rid of such feelings and determine your self-esteem through the word of God. Do not use material things to decide who you are. Your self-esteem should be rooted in who God says you are.

THE PURPOSE OF WEALTH

What is the purpose of wealth according to scriptures? It is for you to be comfortable in the fulfillment of His covenant with you. God wants you materially blessed.

The covenant He made with Abraham which you are enjoying says in Genesis 12:3 that God will bless you and make you a blessing and in you all the families of the earth will be blessed. That is the point. God wants you personally blessed, but beyond that, He needs this money to get other people delivered from the clutches of sin.

God is not an erratic God who does not know what it takes to communicate the gospel to people. He knows prayer and fasting is necessary but that is not all. When Coca Cola wants to sell its products, it gets on the television, radio and newspapers or erects billboards. It paints people's kiosks and the signboards of schools. It sponsors popular events. When the church wants to communicate the gospel to people, we go into prayer and fasting. People know more about Coca Cola than they know about the gospel of our Lord Jesus Christ. Why? We are not speaking where we are supposed to speak. If the Coca Cola advert is on the billboard then a billboard with the message of the gospel should be beside it.

Let people have a choice. Let them have options. But all they see are cigarette adverts. Every thirty minutes they see a cigarette advert on the television. We need to be there too. We need to be on satellite.

In our home we view a Christian channel via satellite. I would rather keep that permanently on and let my children watch that, rather than let them sit in front of a stupid program or watch a video where they are chanting incantations or showing pornographic films. Children absorb these things like sponges.

The main purpose of wealth is to spread the gospel around the world. However, because of greed, God has a big challenge in getting Christians to release money after He has blessed them with it. And you know, when Jesus loves you He will do to you what He did to that young man in the scriptures especially when he sees greed trying to hold you. He will ask you to give everything you have.

How do you break the spirit of greed? That is what Jesus tried to teach the young man in Mark 10. It is by giving, sacrificial giving especially.

*THE MAIN
PURPOSE OF
WEALTH IS TO
SPREAD
THE GOSPEL
AROUND THE
WORLD.*

Give! I have seen some Christians blessed and it is because they broke free from the spirit of greed. They gave. There are Christians who give sacrificially only when pledges are raised in church, but there are some who give sacrificially consistently.

Listen, to break free from the spirit of greed, make your account available to God. Be God's money missionary. In Mark 10 after that young man walked away, Jesus now said, "listen, anybody who gives anything for my sake and the gospel's sake will receive a hundredfold in this world." That is what the young man missed. You can never out-give God.

Greed was the real issue with the rich man who went to hell in Luke16. It was greed that took him there. The poor man who went to heaven did not go there because he was poor. He went there because he was righteous even though he was poor. He was qualified, so he went to heaven. Not all poor people in this world will go to heaven. In fact many poor people will go to hell. There are rich people that will go to hell but then there are lots of rich people who will go to heaven.

"He also said to his disciples, there was a rich man who had a steward and an accusation was brought to him that this man was wasting his goods."[3]

The rich man here is God and the steward is you. The Holy Spirit says to tell you that what He is sending into your life is not yours. It is His own. There was a man in Luke 12 who made the big mistake of thinking it was his. The Bible tells his story from verse 16.

His farm brought forth plentifully and he said to himself, "what will I do now?" He said "I will pull down my barns and build bigger ones and then I will store all my crops and my goods then I will say to my soul, soul eat drink and be merry." That night the Lord spoke to him and said, "You fool, tonight your soul will be required of you then whose will all those things be that you stacked up?" Jesus concluded the story: "so is everyone who is rich towards himself and not towards God."[4]

"I will pull down my barns and build bigger ones, I will store all my crops and my goods then I will say to soul…"[5]

Notice from the passage that there was no God in his speech. Everything was his: the barns, the crops, and the goods. He even said his soul was his own. That was when God decided to take his soul to see who would own everything he had acquired. Jesus taught the same thing in a different way in Luke 16. You are just a steward. Your time, money and energy are not yours. There are people who have worked harder than you and who do not have anything close to what you have. It is God's blessing on what you are doing that is making the difference. The God who gave it to you should be able to demand for it at anytime.

AVOID WASTE

The Spirit of God wants me to tell you that you must fight waste of any sort if you do not want the devil to bring an accusation against you before God. God hates waste. The day Jesus performed the miracle of multiplying the five loaves and two fishes; he said they should gather the fragments so that nothing will be wasted. After gathering the fragments, they had twelve baskets.

The reason for the poverty of some is the fragments they are wasting away. This whole miracle started with just five loaves and two fishes, but at the end of the day, the leftover put them in a better position than they were before the miracle.

When Christians want financial miracles, they make God go back to the same spot over and over again. But it will be easier to feed a crowd with twelve baskets than with five loaves and two fishes. So, take care of the little fragments. Before you get more income, check your outflow. And if you want to control your outflow, the first thing you have got to do is write down every amount of money you spend everyday. It will give you a picture of where your spending is directed.

"He also said to his disciples, there was a rich man who had a steward and an accusation was brought to him that this man was wasting his goods. So he called him and said what is this I hear about you? Give an account of your stewardship for you can no longer be steward."[6]

The Holy Spirit says I should tell you that your stewardship could be terminated at any time. The God who is causing it to flow can stop the flow if you are not going to use it for its divinely ordained purpose. Some reasons why it could be terminated are: refusing to tithe or give offerings, ignoring His instructions when He tells you to give someone some money, to bless a man of God or to give your car to a missionary. If He is unable to get your attention, He says your stewardship could be terminated.

Giving is the key to overcoming greed,. No matter how wealthy you become, always be open and available to God. According to reports, Bill Gates gives an average of three million U.S dollars per day to charity. He believes he is holding the money in trust for the poor of the earth. Most of the money goes into funding research for incurable diseases especially in Africa and Asia. That is someone who understands the purpose of money. The gospel could make do with some money too.

Do not get to the point where you rely so much on the money you have stacked up in your account that God cannot ask you for it. Doing that will prove that you are in the grip of greed. Become God's money missionary. The greatest proofs of your freedom from greed are your investments in the kingdom of God. You must have a testimony like Peter, "we have left all and followed you." (Mark10:28) Sacrificial giving is the key to the one-hundred-fold blessing.

NO MATTER HOW WEALTHY YOU BECOME,
ALWAYS BE OPEN AND AVAILABLE TO GOD

ACTION PLAN

Change your mindset about rich people or about being rich. Poor, short, tall, light, dark, intelligent or stupid people also go to hell and heaven. Heaven is not the exclusive right of the poor. It is the exclusive right of those who have accepted Jesus as their Lord and personal savior. The rules for being rich and for going to heaven are different.

1. Is God part of your life?

....

What is the 'G' factor?

....
....

2. Does God have control over your wealth?

....
....

3. How are the poor supposed to be treated?

....
....

4. List out three (3) things you will spend your money on if you will not have to give account of your spending.

....

....

....

5. What is your response to this adage "A bird in hand is worth two in the bush"?

....

....

....

6. Can you leave what you have now to go in pursuit of something better, based on a promise?

....

7. How will you handle greed?

....

....

....

8. How do you see money?

....

....

....

9. What position do you place money in your life?

....

....

10. How do you spend your money? Let us find out.
Write down every amount of money you spend everyday.
This will show you the direction of your spending.

CHAPTER
7
FINANCIAL EMPOWERMENT

Money is not the root of all evil as it has often been said. You should understand the impact poverty has made on our society. A lot of us came from poor or average backgrounds; hence we have developed a negative mentality about money. This has gotten to the extent that the church has embraced such mentalities and have even found scriptures to support it.

"The love of money is the root of all evil."[1]

In a bid to justify poverty, the scripture has been misquoted to say that money is the root of all evil. The Bible never said that. Money is not the root of all evil, rather the lack of money is the root of most evil. Just look at Africa, and the poor countries of the world. It is so obvious that you do not need anybody to tell you that the lack of money breeds evil. Why is the life expectancy lower in poor countries? Life expectancy is the number of years you are expected to live under normal circumstances. When you check the life expectancy in different countries, you will realize that it is a direct reflection of the economic situation. The circumstances that kill people in developing countries do not kill that easily in developed countries.

Sometimes, we should lay more emphasis on curing poverty than sickness because many diseases are caused by poverty. Psychiatrists have more cases to deal with when there is an economic depression. People have problems because there is so much pressure on their emotions. Even the political system has problems because of poverty.

People vie for political offices, not to serve, but to alleviate once and for all their poverty problems.

IS MONEY GOOD OR EVIL?

Money is not the root of all evil. There are a lot of good things money can do. Money puts good food on your table, clothes you, your children and your spouse. It procures you a good house to live in. According to the Bible, money is a defense.

Nothing will take the place of money in its arena of operation. You cannot go to the store or open market and speak in tongues to the cashier or the market woman as a form of payment. The store/ market security will come after you in moments!

Money is essential. Statistics gathered in the United States show that over 50 per cent of divorce cases are a direct result of money problems.

Money does many good things. There are people who have made a lot sacrifices for us, whom we would really like to reward, if we had the money.

You should change the mind-set that people who have money are evil. Anger directed against rich people is unnecessary. That was the problem with the man who went to hide his talent in the parable. He was angry with his boss.

There are good people who have a lot of money. If you program it into your mind that only thieves and crooks have money, then your spirit will not cooperate with you to get it. When opportunities and ideas come for you to get money, your spirit will reject them. Believe that there are good people who have money and that you are now one of them. Money is neither good nor bad. It is neither immoral nor moral. It is amoral. It takes on the character of the person who has it. The money in the hand of a drug peddler is bad money. However, if he gives me a million dollars today; as soon as it crosses over, it becomes good money. The money would not drag me to the heroin joint and make me sniff heroin. Rather, I would be the one that takes it to the church. As soon as it gets to me, it becomes born-again and Spirit-filled! We will put it to good use in the kingdom of God.

YOU DESERVE TO BE RICH

Also, settle it in your mind that you deserve to be rich. Money is not the exclusive preserve of certain people. The fact that it may have been difficult to obtain money in the past does not imply that you are not entitled to it. God did not make some people more special than you are. All of us are of the same value to God. Put the same value on yourself that God has placed on you.

SETTLE IT IN YOUR MIND THAT YOU DESERVE TO BE RICH.

One of my associates gave this illustration. If there are two hundred naira notes, and one is crispy new while the other is worn and tattered, which would be considered to have more value? Well, someone may conclude that the new one has a higher value, but the truth is they have the same value.

The new note cannot buy more than what the old note would buy in the market. The problem with the old note is that on the outside it has been battered and tattered. It does not reflect its value anymore, but that does not diminish its value. The moral is that all human beings are exactly the same even if we look different on the outside because of what we have gone through.

So do not knock yourself down or write yourself off. It is important that you maintain your self-esteem and call yourself what God has called you. You are not inferior and you deserve to be financially blessed.

Rich people do not have two heads, four ears, forty legs, or four hands. Just as you possess what they have in the physical, your spirit is as valuable as their spirits. The blood Jesus shed on the cross of Calvary for them is the same one He shed for you. Before you were born, the same provision God made for them was made for you. There was no special provision made for anybody.

Of course, they may have stumbled on some things and learned a few secrets that helped them. You deserve to get those things as well and you will obtain them in Jesus name.

MONEY IS NOT SCARCE

Another important mind-set you need to develop is that there is no shortage of money. Shortage is artificial. Some people want to retain their domination over everyone and so create artificial scarcity; but know that there is nothing God created that can ever be in short supply. God is a God of abundance and everything He created is in abundance.

He is El-Shaddai, the multi-breasted God, and the God that is more than enough, the all sufficient God, the omni-potent. He has the potential for everything. If you want something and you ask for it, He will give it to you.

Everything was created in abundance. Any scarcity in the world is artificial so that the world's economic system can keep running. God's economic system is different. It does not run on scarcity. Some countries store or destroy surplus food every year just to keep the prices stable in the world market. Oil cartels regulate the production of oil to keep the prices up. But really, there is no shortage anywhere. We are sitting on a sea of oil.

There is no shortage of money anywhere. If you believe there is an abundance of it available to you, you will begin to see it coming into your life. Why some do not see it flow in their direction is because they do not believe it is available to them.

PROVISION IN REDEMPTION

It is time for you to begin to see money flowing in your direction. God wants you to prosper, believe it. One of the reasons Jesus died for you on the cross is to free you from poverty. Jesus opened the Bible and began to read,

"The spirit of the Lord God is upon me, for He has anointed me to preach the gospel, to the poor."[2]

The first problem Jesus declared that He was sent to solve was that of poverty. You should note that. He said His anointing was first to solve the problem of poverty, then sickness and emotional bondage. It is God's priority that you prosper and be blessed.
"You know the Grace of our Lord Jesus Christ, how that though He was rich, yet for your sakes He became poor that you might become rich."[3]

"You" in this verse refers to you and not someone else. He died on the cross for you to be rich. It will be a colossal waste for Him to have become poor because of you and yet you remain poor. If He made the provision for you and I to be rich, then we should be rich. We may meet obstacles and barriers on the way, but we will bring every one of them down! We will take what belongs to us.

When God symbolically brought Israel out of Egypt, financial wealth was part of the package of their redemption.

"He also brought them forth, with silver and with gold and there was none feeble among all their tribes.[4]

Why didn't He bring them out of Egypt empty handed? Because financial and material wealth will always be part of the redemption package. It will be frustrating for God to solve the sin problem and leave poverty out since the root of poverty is sin. There was no poverty in the world until sin came. How then could God remove sin out of your life and leave poverty? If the sin that brought the poverty has been removed then it is logical that poverty has been annihilated.

When God brought his people out of slavery, lack and bondage, wealth was transferred to them through the blood splashed on doorposts. They plundered Egypt. The New Covenant has an even better package.

Read Deuteronomy 28:1-13 and you will understand that most of the blessings pronounced for obedience have to do with financial and material blessings. When He says these blessings will run after you and overtake you in the land of promise, He is referring to material possessions.

When He says you will be blessed in the house and in the field, He is referring to financial blessings. When He says that the heavens will bring the rain upon your land in due season, it is about financial blessings. When He says (in verse 13) that God will make you the head and not the tail and put you above and not beneath, He is talking about finances. When you are the head, you are in control. When Moses wrote that, he had the picture of a cattle in mind. The head of the cattle decides where the whole cattle goes and the tail does not have a choice. It has to go where the head directs it to go. God will put you in control. But if you lack money, how much can you be in control?

"The poor man's wisdom is despised and his voice is not heard"[5]

FINANCIAL INFLUENCE

Who would listen to a poor church? That is why God has to bless His church. Egypt would not have been bothered if Israel went out empty-handed. Israel wrecked their economy. We need to do something to the economy of our nations, otherwise they would not take us seriously. The things we need to capture their attention require money.

Since most people are not spiritual, they do not care whether you speak in tongues or not. They understand the language of money and what money can do. If money was evil, I believe the devil would have loaded all the different currencies of the world in trucks and dumped them in the different churches.

The devil wants us to perish, so he would want us to have the evil things. Money is not evil. The devil knows that when money gets into the hands of believers who know what to do with it, he is in trouble. That is why he does not even want us to talk about it in church.

...WHEN YOU HAVE MONEY, YOU HAVE OPTIONS.

When you do not have money you do not have a choice. You have to take whatever is given to you. You have to manage whatever comes your way. But when you have money, you have options.

MONEY FLOWS IN THE DIRECTION OF POWER

The crux of this message is that spiritual power is the basic requirement. If you eliminate this from the whole equation, you have missed out on everything. Get the power. Money flows in the direction of spiritual power.

"You shall remember the Lord, your God, because it is He that gives you the power to get wealth."[6]

He won't give you cash directly. If you are looking unto God to give you money, you are still operating at the lower level. All you need is power to command the flow of the cash. The power to get wealth.

Some believe the important thing is capital and they say, "Oh, if I had the capital to do it, I would have made much progress financially."

But, if capital was the most important requirement, God would have said, "I am the one who gives you the capital to get wealth." Some say it is their lack of connections. Then He would have said "I am the one who gives you connections to get wealth." But He said power, because He knows that if you have the power, you will have the wealth, the capital and the connections.

"He called the twelve disciples and gave them power over unclean spirits to cast them out and to heal all manner of sicknesses and diseases."[7]

In verse 4, it says; "And He told them take no purse." Jesus said, "Take no money." I consider this a tough situation. Jesus sent His associates to villages and towns for ministry without money or any other material support. You know, if Jesus had done that in this present day, he would have been considered a wicked senior pastor. However, it was done deliberately so that the disciples could develop confidence in the power of God. Once they had the power, they would get the money and they would get the people.

I also read in Luke 10: 1 about how Jesus called the seventy and sent them out also two by two and told them the same thing.

"And He said to them, 'when I sent you without moneybags, knapsacks and sandals' did you lack anything? They said, 'nothing.'"[8] This implies that the power attracted the provision.

THE BLESSING

When the Bible says you are blessed, it simply means that you are endued with this power.

This power is invisible, but it can rest on your life and cause God's supernatural ability to come on your natural abilities, causing you to produce supernatural results.

This was what happened when Abraham, Isaac and Jacob were blessed. It therefore follows that since you are blessed you should enjoy similar results. The blessing is not the material things you have. Having material things is a result of being blessed.

When you are blessed, people see the effect. When things happen consistently in your life that are positive, people know that there must be something on you. The curse is the direct opposite of the blessing. It produces negative results consistently in a person's life. It is a supernatural force that disrupts the ability to be prosperous. There is also something behind the person that gets good results the blessing, the power to get wealth. God told Abraham:

"I will make you a great nation, I will bless you and make your name great and you shall be a blessing and I will bless those who bless you and curse those who curse you. In you all the families of the earth shall be blessed."[9]

At the time God spoke this to Abraham, nothing had changed in his life physically, but spiritually the atmosphere of his life changed. When God spoke, the power to accomplish greater things came on Abraham. He got it. The Bible goes further to say that he departed as the Lord had spoken to him. In the natural nothing changed, but something had entered into his spirit and that thing became so real to him that he ordered his life around it. He moved and was ready to let go of his accomplishments in the natural because what this power was going to bring was much more than he had already achieved. This is powerful.

The power was released again when God swore the day Abraham offered Isaac. He said:

"By Myself I have sworn..., in blessing I will bless you, and multiplying I will multiply your descendants..."[10]

This is a release of the power to prosper. When Abraham got the power in Genesis 12, he overcame the power of famine and poverty as it is recorded in chapter 13. There was a famine and Abraham went into Egypt with this anointing.

The Bible says by the time he came back, it was with silver and gold, cattle and livestock.

"Then Abram went up from Egypt, he and his wife and all that he had, and Lot with him, to the South. Abram was very rich in livestock, in silver and in gold."[11]

This same power eventually overcame barrenness for Abraham and Sarah, even though they had reached the point where it was impossible for them to have children again. But this power was so strong that at the age of ninety, Sarah gave birth to a child. This power will work in your life also. You will know that it has come upon you, and your life will never remain the same again.

Isaac got the power. Abraham left an inheritance for Isaac. This inheritance was multi-dimensional. There was the material part and the blessing part. Abraham left everything he had for Isaac.

In Genesis 26, another famine struck which was different from the one in the days of Abraham. However, this famine could not wipe away the power Isaac inherited. When Isaac stayed in obedience to God's words in Gerah, he sowed in that land that year and reaped a hundred fold, to the extent that the inhabitants envied him. What was the difference, since he sowed what the inhabitants sowed? There was a supernatural virtue that entered his own seeds and made them produce like no one else's. We need this power. With it we will break the back-bone of poverty in our world. I declare by faith that you will be one of the wealthiest people to ever live in this world because of the insights you have obtained from this book.

Get the power. You know that even Isaac and Rebecca had a problem with barrenness but this power eventually enabled Rebecca to conceive twins. It is the anointing that destroys the yoke. "It shall come to pass in that day, that his burden will be taken away from your shoulder, and his yoke from your neck, and the yoke will be destroyed because of the anointing oil."[12]

The yoke of poverty and barrenness can be destroyed. Power is the key.
I noticed an interesting experience about Ishmael. When Sarah was displeased with Hagar and sent her away, God said to Abraham,

"Do not let it be displeasing in your sight because of the lad or because of your bondwoman. Whatever Sarah has said to you, listen to her voice; for in Isaac your seed shall be called. Yet I will also make a nation of the son of the bondwoman, because he is your seed. So Abraham rose early in the morning, and took bread and a skin of water, and putting it on her shoulder, he gave it and the boy to Hagar, and sent her away. Then she departed and wandered in the Wilderness of Beersheba. And the water in the skin was used up, and she placed the boy under one of the shrubs. Then she went and sat down across from him at a distance of about a bow-shot; for she said to herself, 'let me not see the death of the boy.' So she went and sat opposite him, and lifted her voice and wept."[13]

Obviously, Hagar did not realize that Ishmael had the power. God had pronounced the Word on Ishmael. In Genesis 13, God had told Abraham that He would also make Ishmael a nation. Hagar thought the boy would die because there was no water, no food and no money. However, an anointed man or woman does not die that way.

"God heard the voice of the lad. Then the angel of God called to Hagar out of heaven, and said to her, 'What ails you, Hagar? Fear not, for God has heard the voice of the lad where he is. 'Arise, lift up the lad and hold him with your hand, for I will make him a great nation. And God opened her eyes, and she saw a well of water. Then she went and filled the skin with water, and gave the lad a drink.[14]

Notice that in spite of the fact that it was both Hagar and the boy that were crying, it was the voice of the boy that God heard. The blessing was at work.

Notice also that Abraham gave them food, but this got finished. There is no material thing that anybody can give you that will last you a lifetime. One thing that guarantees your continual prosperity is the power.

The anointing for prosperity was already on the boy.

Hagar was crying instead of tying her destiny to that of the boy. That boy could not have died. There is no way God will say He would make a nation out of someone and then allow the person to die prematurely.

In the natural, water may be used up, but when you have the blessing, your well can never run dry. There are people who are carrying spiritual wells around, but their eyes need to be opened just like Hagar's. Blessed people carry around the potential for wealth and prosperity.

"Blessed are those who dwell in your house. They will still be praising you. Blessed is the man whose strength is in you, whose heart is set on pilgrimage. As they pass through the Valley of Baca, they make it a spring. The rain also covers it with pools. They go from strength to strength every one of them appears before God in Zion."[15]

There are people who by merely passing through the valley of Baca, turn it into a pool. I learnt this a long time ago. The position does not make a man. It is the man that makes the position. No matter what title you give certain people, they empower that title, because the anointing is upon them.

Joseph was that kind of man. He carried an anointing because God spoke to him. When he got to Potiphar's house, he was a slave. But the anointing has no respect for whatever title you are called. It was recorded that the Lord was with Joseph and he was successful to the extent that his master saw him and committed everything he had into his hand (Genesis 39:2.). When he got into prison, the anointing lifted Joseph beyond the position of a prisoner and the warder had to commit the prison affairs into his hands. There is power in the anointing. Get the anointing first.

You have the real thing too. You only need to activate it. From today, wherever you are, your wealth will also be there. You do not need to look for it all over the place. I made up my mind a long time ago when I understood the power in the anointing that it does not matter what title you give me; whatever you call me or wherever you put me, once I occupy an office, my results will be powerful. I am the one who defines the value of the title and the position. The same raw material used to make a Kerosene stove is the one used to make cars. But a Jaguar car is more valuable than a stove. The anointing makes the difference.

"But you have an anointing from the Holy One and you know all things."[16]

When you have this power on you, you will never be at a loss for ideas you need to get what you want. The anointing comes with wisdom. From today, as this power works in you, you will never be stuck again for the rest of your life.

POINTS OF CONTACT FOR THE POWER

There are some contact points for power. Although they may look like religious routines, you should not take them lightly.

1. The blood covenant. This is an agreement in which the blood of two people is mixed together. In this covenant, whatever threatens one of the parties threatens the other. One is under obligation to defend the other.

Whatever belongs to one belongs to the other.

God entered into covenant with man so that our lives could be mixed with His. Whatever threatens us threatens God. Wherever they call your name, God is under obligation to answer on your behalf. Whatever belongs to God, belongs to you.

There is no occult group that initiates people without blood. This is because the devil has no other principles to work with apart from the ones he steals and perverts from God's kingdom. It is a principle. You do not get spiritual power without a blood covenant. That is what the Bible is all about, the Old and New Covenants.

I enjoin you to be a covenant woman and man. Fulfill your part. God is too faithful to break His covenant. When God's blood is running through your veins, you are naturally supernatural and supernaturally natural. You carry God around. That is why God had to change Abraham's name when He entered into covenant with him. Abraham could not remain natural after his encounter with God. As God's power works in you, you will break the barriers that your natural abilities could not break. You will begin to attract the things you could not attract before. Just keep your part. Obey the Word.

2. Worship: coined from the words "worth" and "ship."

It means to tell God what He means to you. When you worship God, you ultimately derive whatever value you want from God. Do not derive your personal value from position, money or other people. There is a connection between worship and wealth. Satan asked Jesus to worship him in exchange for wealth. Christ insisted He would only worship the Father. The first time worship occurred in the Bible was when God was called Jehovah Jireh, the Lord our Provider.[17] When you worship God, you swim in revelations and enjoy mysterious supplies.

3. Prayer: Pray till God speaks to you. Pray till the heavens open over your head. Ask God to show you something new.[18] Pray till your emotions change from negative to positive. Do not waste your fasting or prayer.

Stay in God's presence and let Him speak to you. Until prayer changes you, it would not change your situation.

4. The Word: Acts 20:32 says "I commend you to God and to the word of His grace, which is able to build you up and give you an inheritance among all those who are sanctified."
What you are looking for is in the Word. Spend time in the Word. Listen to tapes. Meditate on the Bible. Your success is tied to it. Stay in the Word until you get a personal revelation and it changes you. The power flows through the Word.

5. Giving: Malachi 3: 10 says; "Prove me now says God, bring your tithes and offerings, let there be meat in My house and see if I will not open for you the windows of heaven and pour you out a blessing"

God says He will pour out a blessing, not money. You may be looking in the wrong place if after giving your tithe, your only expectation is that someone would come and give you money. What you really get is the anointing. God said you will get "a blessing" such that your storehouse will not be able to contain what would flow into your life. Giving is the key. Give tithes. Give offerings and give to kingdom projects. Whenever God asks a man of God to raise offerings for special projects, someone's lifting is usually attached to it. Give to special projects to attract a special anointing.

Give to men of God. The anointing you respect is the anointing you attract. People rub shoulders with men of God without tapping the grace on their lives. You draw the grace on a man of God by listening to and applying his wisdom.

Jesus said in John 6:63, "The words that I speak unto you, they are spirit and they are life." Listen to their tapes until the spirit on the tape enters into your spirit.

Give to the poor. If you give to the poor, your life will rise from obscurity and get to the point where your darkness will be like the brightness of the noon-day. It means the maximum outside will be your own minimum

6. Impartation. Someone who is carrying the power can impart it to you. Matthew 10:1 says;

"And He gave them power…" "And Joshua the son of Nun, was full of the spirit of wisdom, because Moses had laid hands on him."[19]

When you have the power to get wealth, you will never be broke again. If you lose all the material things you have, your heart will not be broken because you have the anointing to reproduce all that was lost and much more. The Spirit of the Lord is upon you because He has anointed you to get wealth, to preach the good news to the poor. You have the power to prosper, to attract wealth. You will never be broke again for the rest of your life. Money and all material things will begin to flow in your direction.

ACTION PLAN

Money is neither good nor bad. It is neither immoral nor moral. It is amoral. It takes on the character of the person who has it.

1. List your present strengths and weaknesses concerning money.

....

....

....

2. How can you move from weakness to strength?

....

....

3. Identify a rich person in your vicinity, area or nation.

....

4. List out the traits you have in common with him.

....

....

....

5. What does he have that you do not have?

....

.

....

6. Has it affected your life in anyway? Why? Or why not?

....

.

....

....

7. Develop a new mindset about money.

CHAPTER
8
RELEASING YOUR INCREASE

❝The path of the just is like the shining sun that shines ever brighter to the perfect day."[1]

"But we all, with unveiled face, beholding as in a mirror the glory of the Lord, are being transformed into the same image from glory to glory, just as by the Spirit of God."[2]

It is your destiny to increase with the passage of time. God expects you to increase. The first thing God said to Adam and Eve was, "be fruitful and multiply." God has invested a lot in nature that commands geometric progression, which is about multiplication and not addition.

Addition is merely an arithmetic progression. I looked through my Bible and I observed that God was consistently saying "You will multiply." Let us look at a few of them:

"I will multiply your descendants exceedingly, so that they shall not be counted for multitude."[3]

"And I will make My covenant between Me and you, and will multiply you exceedingly."[4]

"By Myself I have sworn, says the Lord, because you have done this thing, and have not withheld your son, your only son, in blessing I will bless you, and in multiplying I will multiply your descendants as the stars of the heaven and as the sand which is on the seashore and your descendants shall possess the gates of their enemies."[5]

"And He will love you and bless you and multiply you; He will also bless the fruit of your womb and the fruit of your land, your grain and your new wine and your oil, the increase of your cattle and the offspring of your flock, in the land of which He swore to your fathers to give you."[6]

And when your herds and your flocks multiply, and your silver and your gold are multiplied, and all that you have is multiplied."[7]

"Then out of them shall proceed thanksgiving and the voice of those who make merry; I will multiply them, and they shall not diminish; I will also glorify them and they shall not be small."[8]

You cannot be the child of a big God and remain a small child. Let thanksgiving proceed from you. He will multiply you and you will not diminish. You will progress and not regress. You will increase and not decrease.

When you study the scriptures on multiplication and increase, one common word you will see is seed. "I will multiply your seed." The seed controls the law of multiplication.

"Now, may he who supplies seed to the sower and bread for food, supply and multiply the seed you have sown and increase the fruit of your righteousness.[9]

You cannot talk of fruitfulness without seed. When God said "Be fruitful and multiply," He knew that it would not be morally just to ask Adam and Eve to be fruitful if they were not "seed-full." There cannot be fruits if there are no seeds. If God created the first generation of fruits without putting seeds in them, there would be no fruits in the future. He would have to create fruits everyday.

You need to understand that God has designed life in such a way that we would not have to struggle to flow along with Him. God decided from the beginning that He would not be creating fresh fruits daily. He simplified His job by placing seeds in every fruit, knowing that the seeds would eventually produce fruits when we sow them. He designed it such that if you plant just one seed, the harvest would be more than the previous seed.

The seed principle is powerful. He even determined the future of the human race by the power of the seed. He knew He wanted billions of people on the earth, but decided to create just two.

If the human destiny is controlled by the power of the seed, then everything else is controlled by the power of the seed. If you get a good hold of the seed principle, your future is guaranteed, because that is where God invested the future.

Many people do not recognize the answers to their prayers. They keep asking God for a harvest when God has given them the seed. They despise and ignore the seed, not realizing that what they are expecting is in the seed. Two kinds of seeds control your financial destiny.

SPIRITUAL SEEDS

This refers to the Word of God. In the parable of the sower, Jesus said the seed is the Word of God. The state of your heart will always control your situation on the earth. The Bible says, "As he thinks in his heart, so is he." Your natural seeds would not produce beyond the degree to which your spiritual seeds are producing in your heart. The starting point is to allow the seed of God's Word to be planted in your heart. If you want to operate with spiritual power and prosper through God's spiritual resources, let the word grow and bring forth spiritual fruits in your heart.

"You will prosper and be in health even as your soul prospers."[10]

FINANCIAL SEEDS

The natural seed that controls your financial destiny is the money you have now. The seeds of the present control the future. The law of multiplication is a death and resurrection experience. Until your seed dies, it would not grow. That is why your seed decays when you first plant it in the soil. You may understand that your seed controls your destiny, but until you sow the seed, you would not get a harvest. If you decorate the seed, the only thing you will have is just your decorated seed. It will not in anyway affect your destiny. Jesus said,

"Except a grain of wheat falls to the ground and dies, it abides alone, but if it dies, it brings forth much fruit."[11]

The seed needs to die.

The resurrected version is always the glorified form of the one that died. The Jesus that resurrected was not the one that died. The one that died could not walk through walls. But, after He resurrected, He could. He died in weakness, but resurrected, in power.

When seeds die, their old coverings disintegrate and God covers them with new flesh.

For example, when Christians die their bodies decay, but when

Jesus shows up in the skies and the trumpet of God sounds, the Bible says that those who have died in Christ will resurrect first with bodies better than the ones we have now. The bodies we will resurrect with will have power over the laws of gravity. The body we carry now is still plagued by sickness, but sickness will not be able to hold down resurrected bodies.

Always bear it in mind that the harvest can never be the same as the seed that was sown. You should understand that God will not take something from you and let it come back the same way.

He took a bone from Adam and replaced it with a decorated bone called a woman. She was so beautiful that Adam screamed, "Wow man!" when he saw her. So, recognize that your future is trapped in your seed. If you keep your seed, that is the most it will be; but if you sow it that is the least it will be. Always maintain this attitude toward your seed.

CONTROL THE FUTURE

The future is in the seed. God wanted billions of humans on the earth, yet in His infinite wisdom, He decided that there would be no point having to breathe into the soil again anytime a new man was to be created. Instead, He created the man and the woman and put the seeds in man, so that billions of human beings can come from the seed. If you do not mind your seeds, you are not minding your future. Since the future is in the seed, you take your future only as seriously as you take your seeds.

In the area of finances, Christians want God to perform great wonders. Imagine a couple that just got married, always praying together and trusting God for a child, yet, never have intercourse. Even if they prayed until "kingdom come," they would still not have a child. The only virgin that ever got pregnant was Mary and we are not expecting another Jesus.

If you apply this illustration to finances, you will realize where the problem lies with Christians who pray fervently for a harvest without planting. Such Christians leave the seeds to waste, not realizing that the power of multiplication is in the seed.

YOU REAP WHAT YOU SOW

Always understand that the kind of seed you sow is the kind of harvest you will reap. When you pray, what you get is spiritual.

Always bear it in mind that the harvest can never be the same as the seed that was sown.

Dr. Robert Schuller said, "Sow a prayer and reap an idea." Many people do not receive the answers to their prayers because they do not understand what God gives from the realm of the spirit. There is no money in heaven. They neither spend dollars nor any other currency there, so do not expect any to come from there.
However, whatever is traded in heaven controls and dominates this earth because the invisible world created the physical world. Whatever heaven gives you is intangible and invisible, yet it gives you control of the natural world. When you pray, you receive the anointing, grace, visions, ideas, dreams and revelations. It is these things that control the universe.

In Malachi 3: 10, God promised that if you pay your tithes, He would pour you out a blessing that you will not have enough room to receive. We need to ask questions. I have been paying tithes for about fifteen years. I have never seen money drop down from heaven.

What I am saying then is that when you have sown spiritual seeds into your life, you reap grace, anointing and an increase in the power and wisdom of God in your life. Yet, in the natural, no matter how anointed you are, if you do not sow corn, you cannot reap corn.

In the realm of finances, the natural seed that you sow to enjoy multiplication is the money in your hand. Your future is trapped in your seed.

Dr. Myles Munroe said, "The death of a seed is the burial of a forest." When a seed dies, a future harvest dies.
When a human seed dies in the womb, it is an unquantifiable loss. In parts of the world where abortion is legal, they say that the fetus in the womb is not yet a human being until it is born. But this is a lie. That seed in the womb carries the future. In fact, it is the future. Aborting a pregnancy is killing an engineer, a doctor or the best president a nation may ever have.

If you keep your seed, that is the most it will be. If you sow your seed, that is the least it will be. You can move from where you are to where you want to be if you understand the law of the seed. You can create a future for yourself. If you frame or glaze your seed and put it in the cabinet in your room, that is the way it will remain, and after some time it will die. It is when you sow your seed that it has any possibility of increasing.

"While the earth remains, seedtime and harvest and cold and heat, and summer and winter, and day and night shall not cease"[12]

God said that as long as the earth remains, seed-time and harvest shall never cease. When I studied the seed principle, it helped me take control over my future. It is only through your seed that you can control your future. I decided to sow my seeds in the morning. I may not see any result today, but I know that one day all my fields will be green and it will be harvest season. The time of youth is not the time to play around.

IF YOU KEEP YOUR SEED,
THAT IS THE MOST IT WILL BE.
IF YOU SOW YOUR SEED,
THAT IS THE LEAST IT WILL BE.

In the world, they advice you to "sow your wild oats." I thank God that I found Christ, so I do not have any wild oats to sow. God measures seeds out for everyone for their lives and destinies. I do not have any extra to throw into the wild and waste. My seeds were apportioned for me to sow per time. There is a time to sow and a time to reap.

UNLIMITED INCREASE

Dr. Robert Schuller said, "You can count the number of seeds in an apple, but you cannot count the number of apples in a seed."

When you step into this area of the seed principle, you enter into an unlimited future. Because until Jesus comes and this world disappears, seeds will continue to be multiplied and bring more and more increase. When you understand the seed principle, time works in your favor. If you do not sow your seeds when your contemporaries are sowing theirs, by the time they are reaping, you will be frustrated.

Cocoa is worth more than corn, because it usually takes seven to eight years to harvest cocoa. If you refuse to sow your seeds when others are sowing, when they are reaping, you will realize that what they were doing made sense, even though it appeared stupid at the time. It may then be too difficult for you to start sowing to catch up with them. It may take another seven to eight years for you to start reaping your own.

YOU CAN COUNT THE NUMBER OF SEEDS IN AN APPLE, BUT YOU CANNOT COUNT THE NUMBER OF APPLES IN A SEED.

My advice to you is that however late it is, start now. That is the only way you can break the power of lack and poverty in your life. If you do not start now, the longer you wait to sow your seed, the poorer you become because you would have delayed your harvest. I pray that you and your children will never beg.

SOW YOUR SEED

"He that observes the wind will not sow, and he who regards the cloud will not reap."[13]

Do not let circumstances dictate what you do. You should not sow seeds only when you feel like sowing.

God did not leave it to your feelings, because He has already determined the seasons. Seedtime and harvest time are determined. If you feel like sowing in the winter, your feelings would have deceived you. Sow when you have to sow. Sow your financial seeds now.

The Holy Spirit spoke to me some years back when my ministry was having some challenges and as a result cut back on our radio broadcasts. We transferred to a station with a cheaper air - time but with a reach not as broad as the previous.

A few months later, the Holy Spirit said He was not behind the transfer, that I had allowed circumstances to affect me. He said anything that forces you to reduce the quality and quantity of seeds you are sowing today has already reduced the quantity of your harvest. Whatever it will take, stay there. You should only increase your seeds, do not cut back.

There is no one who does not have something to sow. The Bible says, "He gives seed to the sower and bread to the eater." There was a time I was not giving offerings in the school fellowship I used to attend because I thought even God knew I did not have anything.

However, with wisdom, I know there is always something to give. It could be a tie, shoes, or television. I have given all kinds of things, and I have discovered that each time I gave, there was a financial shift.

TITHING

Tithe means a tenth. The essence of these financial teachings is to show us that God wants us to put our financial lives in order. One of the uppermost things on God's mind is order because wherever you see order, you will see increase. Sometime ago the Holy Spirit pointed me to an area of my finances and I wrote down some action points. As soon as I made adjustments in those areas, my income appreciated and I saw this as a sign of approval. Order makes way for increase.

If you were asked, and you could not explain on paper what you did with all of your income last month, you are not ready for financial increase. If you cannot show the apportionment and a budget for your income, you are not ready.

Order makes for increase. That is the law in heaven.

Before you were born everything you would ever need was created, so everything you need is around you. They are only in the wrong places. You make progress when you move each thing to its place. Even disorder in the body causes dysfunction, pain and discomfort.

Many of us are experiencing financial pain. Pain is not bad. It is a mechanism God put in the body to help us know if something is wrong. If you are experiencing pain in your finances, something is wrong and all it needs is correction.

Pay your tithes. In Leviticus 27:30, the Bible established the status of the tithe. The tithe is not the pastor's idea.
It reads, "And all the tithe of the land, whether of the seed of the land or of the fruit of the tree, is the Lord's. It is holy to the Lord."

You are not doing God a favor by tithing. It is His. He factored it into your income from the beginning. When Israel was moving into the Promised Land, God told them that the first city they capture would be His. When they gave birth to children the first male would be His. When the cattle gave birth, the first one was His.

The tithe is the proof of your dependence on God; that you have overcome fear and you entrust your future into His hands. It is the proof that you are not self-sufficient. It is like circumcising your money, which purifies the remaining of it.

"Honor the Lord with your possessions and with the first fruits of all your increase.[14]

If you agree that order creates increase, you will agree that the first thing to take out from your income is your tithe. Most times, whatever you list as the last item on your budget does not get funded.

Some look financially prosperous today, but if God is not part of your finances, you are not blessed. Something will be wrong in one area of your life. You may have all the money in the world but have no peace of mind. You need God's blessing and God says the reason why you are not blessed is because you are stealing from Him.

Some think that the tithe is a gift to God. It is not a gift. It is the Lord's. In fact, some people pay tithes and nothing else, especially if it is a high figure. God has already laid claim on your tithe. Every responsible citizen pays tax to the Government, in a lot of cases by direct deductions. However, God gave the believer the privilege of bringing the tithe himself to keep the kingdom going. Stop

THE TITHE IS THE PROOF OF YOUR DEPENDENCE ON GOD.

playing games with God. Stop calculating all kinds of deductions on your income. Some people ask if they should pay tithe on their net or gross income. If you calculate deductions with God, you will have gross problems.

Somebody was trusting God for a promotion and the level he was targeting was three steps ahead so he increased his tithe to reflect the income of the new level. In a few weeks, he was promoted to that level. Spiritual principles are powerful. God wants to prosper you, but He wants you to be in order first.

There was a widow who was paying a dollar tithe, sixteen years later oil was discovered on her land. Some years ago, oil was discovered on a ministry's property. This ministry has given out aircrafts. It is God who put all the minerals in the soil. He said the gold and silver are His. He can position you where money can be found.

OFFERINGS

In addition to the tithe, give offerings. Your giving begins with the offering. Give in such a way that it reflects God's blessings on your life. Some people's offering does not change even when their income increases. Remember that your offering has not started until you pay your tithe. Obedience is better than sacrifice.

Also give to the poor. Deuteronomy 15 says you will always have the poor with you. God said that you should not harden your hearts to the poor amongst your brethren, so that He can bless you.

This is not because God has destined some people to be poor, but because, there will always be people who will disobey God. There will always be people who will be looking for shortcuts. Some prefer waking up in the night to do spiritual warfare but disobeys simple instructions. Yet they will be looking for financial breakthroughs.

There will always be people who will refuse to read books and listen to tapes on finances. So the poor will always be there. God says you should rescue them and for that He will bless you. Have it in your program to pay someone's school fees, someone's rent, or to give scholarships. Minister to the poor. Do not give excuses for not giving.

In Israel, farmers were not allowed to harvest everything. God said they should leave some for the poor. Plan to settle someone's hospital bills, accommodation bills and so on.

Give to special projects. Anytime God calls for special projects, somebody is about to be promoted.

GIVE PASSIONATELY

Be passionate in your giving. In 1 Chronicles 29:1-5,David proved to be a very passionate man. He was raising offering for the building of the temple and he brought out gold, silver, bronze and all sorts of things. In the Dakes Bible, it was estimated that what David gave amounted to $100,000,000 in one day. He said,

"I have set my affection with all of my mind and all that I have on the house of my God."

Be a God lover, a kingdom promoter, a kingdom investor and a kingdom addict. Jesus said,

"Do not lay up your treasure on the earth, where worms and moths can corrupt, rather, lay up your treasure in heaven where thieves cannot break in and things are not corrupted."

As much as you should invest in the stock market, always bear it in mind that it could crash.

We had a special project sometime ago and God gave us a verse of scripture.

"Unless a grain of wheat falls into the ground and dies, it remains alone; but if it dies, it produces much grain."[15]

God told us that except our church died then, a new one would never arise. Our church was in an abandoned building with a shed for extension. I preached a message then titled "I Am More Than

This. " That message came from the depth of my spirit.

Be passionate in your giving.

I would go to the services grieved in my spirit most times. I knew we were not meant for that place. Sometimes, we would be holding a service and the aroma of food would fill the air; or loud music from people whose rooms were joined to our auditorium would interfere with the service.

God advised us to throw ourselves into the offering basket. So people started giving. Cars, microwave ovens, jewelry, shoes, and all kinds of things. The church sold them to raise the money that enabled the Church to move. Everyone that gave at that time can give the testimony of great shifts in their finances.

So, give to special projects. By the time God says "special project" give immediately, because that is why He gave you what you have presently. He could not have asked Israel to build His tabernacle in the wilderness if He had not given them power and favor to collect things free of charge from the Egyptians. When God is blessing you and your business is growing, please understand that He would call on you one day to give out of what He has given you.

GIVE TO MINISTERS OF GOD

Finally, give to men of God. Bless your Pastor. Make provision for this in your income. Do organized giving. It is a spiritual principle and it is one of the major keys God has used to bless me. Melchizedek blessed Abraham, and Abraham gave him his tithes. (Genesis 14: 18-20) Every time spiritual virtue leaves a man of God to you, there should be an exchange.

"Let him who is taught the word share in all good things with him who teaches."[16]

"If we have sown spiritual things for you, is it a great thing if we reap your material things?"[17]

There should be an exchange. I have experienced grace from this principle. Our church has grown to several times its former size in recent years. God's grace on my life has increased. This is the meaning of multiplication. Even our income is not tied to natural laws anymore. God has blessed us anyhow.

"Let him who is taught the word share in all good things with him who teaches. Do not be deceived, God is not mocked; for whatever a man sows, that he will also reap.[18]

This is talking about giving to men of God. Verse 8 says, "For he who sows to his flesh will of the flesh reap corruption, but he who sows to the Spirit will of the Spirit reap everlasting life."

This means that you will have spiritual problems if you eat what God expects you to sow. Verse 9 says;

"And let us not grow weary while doing good, for in due season we shall reap if we do not lose heart."

This entire passage is about sowing into the lives and ministries of men of God.

I have gone to different churches to preach and I have come to the conclusion that when you see a poor pastor, you see a poor congregation and when you see a blessed pastor, you see a blessed congregation. When you keep what God has asked you to give, it creates spiritual problems for you. When you obey God, your return is more than just money. There is a spiritual covering over your family, protection, sound health, and ideas for the growth of your business. I have noticed throughout scriptures that when you give in obedience to God's Word, fresh ideas are released.

Solomon gave a thousand burnt offerings and God showed up in the night and asked him what he wanted.[19]

Jacob vowed to pay tithes and an angel showed up in the night and gave him an idea, which made him more prosperous than his employer.[20]

RECEIVE THE GRACE TO SOW

"No man takes it from Me, but I lay it down of Myself; I have power to lay it down, and I have power to take it again."[21]

Until you have the power to lay it down, you would not get the power to take it up, because you did not sow anything. You can possess your dream and vision if you lay down your seeds. That is how it works in the realm of the spirit. Always remember that what you take up is always more than what you lay down. Each time, giving will move you to a new level.

Ask for grace to continually break your own record in giving. If the Holy Spirit says you should clear your account and give it to the person sitting next to you and you obey, then God knows that anytime He gives an instruction, you will obey. You are then ready to enjoy the fullness of His blessings. It takes God to move people to give to you. For a long time, I never heard about sacrificial offerings in church. That was what Abraham was willing to give when he was to offer Isaac. Since I decided to live permanently on the sacrificial level, God has put me on an irreversible path of financial breakthrough.

The destiny you are looking for is a harvest, what you have today is your seed. If you do not have the power to lay it down, you would not have a harvest. You will watch other people harvest yearly and the fear that is stopping you from obeying God's voice will keep you from your harvest. I pray that this will not be your experience.

The Holy Spirit told me once that anything that pushes you to reduce the quantity of the seed you are sowing today is already reducing the quantity of your harvest in the future.

That changed my mentality so that when I am giving, I am not thinking about the present, but about the future.

Nobody gives beyond the size of their vision.

Do something special as a result of your contact with this book. Make a special investment into God's work today wherever He leads you to do it. Expect a miracle.

I pray that you will receive grace to step into the fullness of the anointing for financial success. God's blessings will run after you and overtake you. God will set you on high above all the nations of the earth. Those who think they have money will see you and they will realize they do not have anything. Receive the anointing to prosper.

ACTION PLAN

* Give thanks all the time for what you have and what you are about to get.

* Identify something you want or someone you desire to be like and, sow a seed for it.
* Do not leave the practical for the spectacular

* Put your ideas into practice. Sow your seed (financial or otherwise) today.

* Pay your tithe (Give 10 per cent of your income to God). Connect with the supernatural blessing.

* Give to the poor, friends, parents, the church, charities and so on.

After you have achieved your financial goals and lived a long healthy life, how do you intend to invest your funds so it will continue to affect lives long after you have left this world?

....

....

Act now. Act fast! You will succeed.

See You At The Top!

SUCCESS POWER

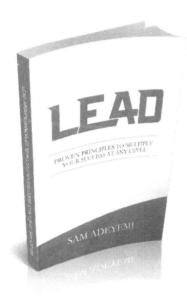

Wherever you are on the success journey, LEAD is the right book for you. It is packed with ideas you can use right away to transform your life right where you are, and it will help you increase your capacity for success in geometric proportions.

In this book, you will learn how to:

- *Unleash your ability to inspire others*
- *Leverage on principles to develop character*
- *Solve problems better and faster than before*
- *Transform your family and organization*
- *Become a change champion in your nation*

FOR OTHER TITLES,
Visit www.samadeyemi.net,
www.successpower.tv

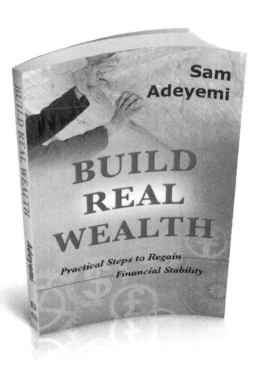

SUCCESS
POWER

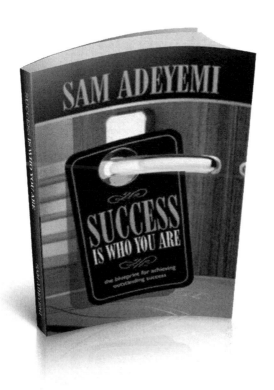

ENDNOTES

Chapter One

1 Matthew 25:14
2 Matthew 25:14
3 Isaiah 48:17
4 Psalm 23:1
5 Psalm 31:15
6 Psalm 90:12
7 Mark 2:22
8 Matthew 25:16
9 Matthew 25:18
10 Matthew 25:23
11 Matthew 25:24
12 Matthew 25:25
13 The Instant Millionaire
by Mark Fisher
14 Matthew 25:26
15 Matthew 25:27
16 Matthew 13:12
17 Matthew 25:30

Chapter Two

1 Proverbs 23:7
2 Proverbs 27:19
3 Matthew 12:35 (AMP)
4 Proverbs 4:23
5 Matthew 9:17
6 Romans 12:2
7 I Timothy 6:10
8 II Corinthians 10:3-5
9 2Kings 5
10 Luke 5:39
11 Proverbs 4:23
12 Proverbs 15:15
13 Deuteronomy 28:47-48
14 Proverbs 29:18
15 Ephesians 3:20
16 Genesis 13:14-15
17 Habakkuk 2:1-2
18 Acts 2:16-17
19 Ephesians 1:18
20 Psalm 103:7

Chapter Three

1 Proverbs 22:7
2 Luke 14: 28-31
3 Isaiah 1:18
4 Exodus 25:8-9
5 Habakkuk 2:2
6 Ecclesiastes 5:11
7 Proverbs 1:5
8 Proverbs 22:29
9 Ecclesiastes 10:10 (NIV)

Chapter Four

1 Proverbs 21:20
2 Proverbs 27:12
3 Joel 2:28
4 James 1:25

Chapter Five

1 Isaiah 1:18-19
2 Habakkuk 2:1
3 Romans 12:3
4 Proverbs 17:8
5 Proverbs 22: 29

Chapter Six

1 1 Timothy 6: 9-10
2 Mark 10:21
3 Luke 16:1
4 Luke 12:21
5 Luke 12 : 18-19
6 Luke 16:1-2

Chapter Seven

1 I Timothy 6:12
2 Luke 4:17
3 II Corinthians 8:9
4 Psalm 105:37
5 Ecclesiastes 9:16

6 Deuteronomy 8:18
7 Matthew 10:1
8 Luke 22:35
9 Genesis 12:2-4
10 Genesis 22:16-17
11 Genesis 13:1
12 Isaiah 10:27
13 Genesis 21:12-16
14 Genesis 21:17-19
15 Psalm 84:4-7
16 I John 2:20
17 Genesis 22:5
18 Jeremiah 33: 3
19 Deuteronomy 34:9

Chapter Eight

1 Proverbs 4:18
2 II Corinthians 3:18
3 Genesis 16:10
4 Genesis 17:2
5 Genesis 22: 16-17
6 Deuteronomy 7:13
7 Deuteronomy 8:13
8 Jeremiah 30:19
9 II Corinthians 9:10
10 III John 2
11 John 12:24
12 Genesis 8:22
13 Ecclesiastes 11:4
14 Proverbs 3:9
15 John 12:24
16 Galatians 6:6
17 I Corinthians 9:11
18 Galatians 6:6-7
19 I Kings 3
20 Genesis 31:9-13
21 John 10:18

30560542R00077

Printed in Great Britain
by Amazon